Liturgical Theology Revisited

Liturgical Theology Revisited

Open Table, Baptism, Church

ψ

Stephen Edmondson

With a Foreword by Phyllis Tickle

Liturgical Theology Revisited

Open Table, Baptism, Church

ψ

Stephen Edmondson

With a Foreword by Phyllis Tickle

CASCADE *Books* · Eugene, Oregon

LITURGICAL THEOLOGY REVISITED
Open Table, Baptism, Church

Cascade Books
An Imprint of Wipf and Stock Publishers
199 W. 8th Ave., Suite 3
Eugene, OR 97401

www.wipfandstock.com

ISBN 13: 978-1-62654-835-8

Cataloging-in-Publication data:

Edmondson, Stephen.

    Liturgical theology revisited : open table, baptism, church / Stephen Edmondson.

    xvi + 148 p. ; 23 cm. —Includes bibliographical references.

    ISBN 13: 978-1-62654-835-8

    1. Lord's Supper (Liturgy). 2. Lord's Supper—Anglican Communion. 3. Closed and open communion. I. Title.

BX5149.C5 E30 2015

Manufactured in the U.S.A.

For Cyndi, a ray of grace

The table of bread and wine is now to be made ready.
It is the table of company with Jesus,
and all who love him.
It is the table of sharing with the poor of the world,
with whom Jesus identified himself.
It is the table of communion with the earth,
in which Christ became incarnate.
So come to this table,
you who have much faith
and you who would like to have more;
you who have been here often
and you who have not been for a long time;
you who have tried to follow Jesus,
and you who have failed;
Come.
It is Christ who invites us to meet him here.

—The Invitation to the Table
from the Iona Abbey Worship Book

Table of Contents

Foreword ix

Acknowledgements xiii

1 Introductions 1

2 Jesus and the Table 21

3 A Theology of the Open Table 54

4 Baptism and the Spirit 84

5 The Church and Its Mission 116

Bibliography 147

Foreword

The twenty-first century was hardly midway through its first decade of life before all our media outlets began to be crowded, almost to the point of tedium, with words and analyses and theoretical explanations about the dramatic shift—occurring then among perfectly ordinary people and still occurring among them today—of personal fealty from organized or traditional religions to nondoctrinal ones and sometimes even to nonsystems themselves. Like some kind of electronic feeding frenzy, everything from individual blogs and less humble podcasts to commercially published books and professionally produced YouTube clips were having their own say and offering their own assessment of the "whys" and the "now whats?" Nor has there ever been any want of academic papers and scholarly commentary on the whole thing, either.

Over the years, some of the scholarly analyses and commentary were, and have continued to be, fairly low-key and helpful, if not encyclopedic. Others, of course, have been eagerly awaited and, almost immediately upon their publication, have proven themselves more than worthy of the wait. Christian Smith's long-anticipated 2014 release, *Young Catholic America: Emerging Adults In, Out of, and Gone from the Church,* is certainly a stellar recent example of that category. But among the whole cache of such anticipated studies, another recent release has proved to be particularly useful and insightful to me.

The book I am referencing is written by Linda Mercadante, who, as B. Robert Straker Professor of Historical Theology at Methodist Theological School, obviously has both the skill and the authority to produce enormously useful and astute commentary. And certainly, the subtitle of Mercadante's groundbreaking volume in this area is cleanly and clearly descriptive of its contents. It reads: *Inside the Minds of the Spiritual But Not Religious.* It is not the subtitle, however, that I find to be most arresting and most memorable; it is Mercadante's title itself that draws me.

FOREWORD

Simple to the point of exquisite precision, that title reads: *Belief Without Borders*. And in those three simple words and their juxtaposing, Mercadante nails it . . . nails the nature of the shifting and exposes the impetus driving it. It is the proprietary borders . . . those old fences and stagnating moats . . . those defining and confining surveyor's stakes and corner markers that are the strangulating problem. But those very things are also family bequests which must be honored, just as they can be neither returned nor unsaid, except . . .

Except, of course, that moats can be cleaned and transformed into bodies of living, moving water that cool the spaces they were originally built to defend. Fences can be repaired—repainted, even—into comfortable, attractive statements of pleasing definition. Borders can be drawn and redrawn without damage to their historic integrity if they are honored in memory and unpunctuated by armed crossing points. Ancient surveyor stakes and corner markers can be raised and then burnished enough to carry with grace and beauty the date of their placement, even as they continue to bear testimony to their role in a land's evolution and its people's history.

In matters of faith, however, moat cleaning and stake raising are not work for an ordinary laborer. Interestingly enough and because of their deeply personal and integral nature, they are not always work best done by academic theologians, either. More often than not, in fact, those tasks are most pastorally and effectually carried out by parish clergy . . . by the men and women who, having had formal theological training, also have in hand the nontheoretical skills of hands-on pastoring, of facing in-your-face anxieties with empathy, and of surviving, with at least a modicum of humor, an almost daily barrage of questions born out of yearning frustrations. In a sense, in other words, it is—and increasingly is going to be—the work of practicing clergy to look to the borders and to the borderlands to discern for parishioners and would-be parishioners and even for the never-want-to-be parishioners what the borders mean, how accurately they have been drawn, how defensible is their current mapping . . .

And of this growing benison, there can be no better or more current example than the book you have in your hands, for the book you have in your hands is written by a clergyman who has also been an academic, and it addresses an increasingly troublesome section of border.

Father Edmonson is an Episcopal priest, and his concern is with the frighteningly divisive issue of the Eucharist and of access to it. Who may come to, and participate in, this most central of the Christian sacramental

x

mysteries? By what process and under what conditions? Is the table of our Lord open to all? Or only to some? If so, to whom? Why, and by whose authority? Is it possible—even probable, perhaps—that Christianity over the centuries has managed to abrade and limit its own inheritance? Has it exchanged the truth of revelation for the security of fixed absolutes? Has it, in sum, managed to create borders for itself that were never part of the territory given?

And if so . . .

. . . And if so, how now shall we worship and believe? How now shall we honor what has been, holding it to our souls in affection and respect? How now shall we grow and change and morph, like every living thing, from what is and has been into what faith is?

If all of the answers to these questions do not reside in these pages— and they do not—then most certainly some of them do. Moreover, such answers as are indeed given here are not merely answers. Rather, they are foundational points for communal prayer and communal discussion. May those of us who enter them, then, enter quietly and thoughtfully, for what- ever else this is that we are entering, it most surely is holy land and hallowed ground.

Phyllis Tickle

Acknowledgements

THIS BOOK IS GROUNDED in the beautiful human reality that we are most truly the people God created us to be as we are for and from each other. This is true of its content, but it is equally true of its author. I want to acknowledge here at the beginning the communities and individuals from whom I have drawn faith, life, and inspiration. They, in many ways, have made this book what it is.

I initially learned of God, grace, and Jesus' love from Mike Macey and the whole community at Trinity Church in Longview, Texas. What I learned of spiritual friendship at All Saints in Palo Alto helped me understand more fully what it meant to receive Jesus' presence in and with the circle of the eucharistic community. Likewise, at St. Cyprian's in Lufkin I learned to see hospitality as a way of living that embraces God's world in its need. I was especially touched by their sense of hospitality as a ministry shared, owned and embodied by all the baptized. In my time with Steve Kelsey and the Middlesex Area Cluster Ministry in Connecticut, I came to appreciate more fully how a deep belief in the Spirit empowering the baptized for ministry equips the church with the needed gifts for its mission.

I first encountered an explicitly open table congregation in the Diocese of Washington at St. Mark's on Capitol Hill. Their life, in many ways, was built around the virtue of eucharistic hospitality. What was most instructive, however, was the pairing of this hospitality with a deep commitment to the Christian community as the place where lives are nurtured and souls deepened. This found particular expression in their emphasis on Christian initiation, their energy for the sacrament of baptism, and their covenant to insist that continued catechesis formed the heart of the Christian life.

Now I am sharing the adventure of the Christian life with St. Thomas' in McLean, as we struggle together to open our lives to God's agenda in the midst of the busyness of Northern Virginia. At St. Thomas' I've experienced profoundly a Christian community defined by its bonds, not it's boundaries. It's the quality of loving relationships in this community that allows it to be a whole-making space. Likewise, the deep commitment to relationship among the people of St. Thomas' has encouraged an understanding of hospitality as much as an act of inclusion and integration as it is an act of welcome.

The power of the movement to open the eucharistic table has been evident to me in the capacity of Christian communities far from my home to have equally shaped me. St. Gregory of Nyssa in San Francisco has always been in the vanguard of the movement to open the table, and the writings of Rick Fabian, Donald Schell, and Sara Miles have seeded much of the theology and spirituality of this book. More importantly to me, the support they have provided to my writing has been a blessing. I am especially thankful for the time Rick Fabian took to compose a most thoughtful critique and challenge to my initial manuscript. His critique aided me in deepening my approach, and I regret I was not able to respond to his thoughtful missive as fully as I might. Donald Schell has, likewise, given me invaluable encouragement and guidance as I have sought to enter the public discourse over the open table.

So, too, the Iona Community in Scotland has taught me much about evangelical hospitality. They express this hospitality in their varied ministries and I was a grateful recipient of it when I visited the abbey on retreat while I was working on this book. More importantly, they have created and shared a rich set of liturgical resources for practicing the hospitality that Jesus preached. Their passion for Jesus' love, evident in so many aspects of their life, comes to poetic expression in these resources.

I may never have begun this book without the support of the Valparaiso Project, which funded my initial study of the practice of the open table. I want to thank the participants in that study, the parishes of St. John's, Norwood; Epiphany, DC; and Trinity, DC, who, along with St. Mark's, provided the original insight into the theological breadth and complexity entailed by the practice of the open table for the life of a Christian community. Likewise I am thankful to the *Anglican Theological Review* and its managing editor, Jackie Winter, for publishing my first musings on this topic.

I am grateful to the faculty and students at the Virginia Theological Seminary, who provided me with friendship and intellectual companionship. In this community, I was able to hone the virtues of intellectual rigor and theological imagination, while being reminded that the best of Christian theology is rooted in Scripture and dedicated to the mission of the church. I especially want to thank Dean Martha Horne for allowing me the year-long sabbatical during which I laid the foundation for this book.

Many other individuals gave me invaluable guidance along the way. Phyllis Tickle gave me feedback on the substance of my work and, perhaps more importantly, gave me direction on how to move from a manuscript to a publication. David and Julie Kelsey offered me close readings of my finished manuscript, helping me to reshape my initial draft into the document you have today. Shannon Craigo-Snell was supportive of my work and pointed me towards Cascade Books as a potential publisher.

You would not be reading this book if Matthew Wimer at Cascade Press had not offered it a publishing home. I am thankful for the careful attention that he and Rodney Clapp have given my work, and for the commitment of Cascade and Wipf and Stock to this work. Kaudie McLean has graced my manuscript with her editorial talents, and I appreciate all of the ways that she has tightened up my prose.

Finally, I must thank my wife, Cyndi, for her love and support through all of my writing, and Andrew and Christopher for the joy and the hope with which they fill my days.

CHAPTER 1

Introductions

And then we gathered around that table. And there was more singing and standing, and someone was putting a piece of fresh, crumbly bread in my hands, saying "the body of Christ," and handing me the goblet of sweet wine, saying "the blood of Christ," and then something outrageous and terrifying happened. Jesus happened to me.

—SARA MILES, *TAKE THIS BREAD*

EVERY NIGHT, OUR FAMILY gathers around the table, and we engage in the ritual of dinner. At the start of the meal, we hold hands and thank God for God's blessings. Sometimes we do this twice, remembering that prayer is not a race and that we don't begin until we're holding hands. We sit and serve the meal. We're reminded to compliment the food and with it the cook. (Mealtime is a ritual of thanksgiving in many ways.) We share our day and learn not to interrupt one another—to be interested and respectful of what everyone is saying. We eat vegetables. Every meal. Everyone. They're healthy for us. We finish our meal and then get a treat (unless we've hit our brother).

I don't know what my children understand about this shared time, or what they've understood about it in the past. I do care that sometime in the future they'll understand what we're doing there at the table, but for now, I'm more focused on what happens there. Thanks is given. Stories are shared. We're each known and recognized. Our bodies are nourished.

Broccoli works—it does its broccoli thing—whether we understand it or not, whether we believe in it or not. (My five-year-old does not believe in broccoli.)

I wish we could welcome more folks, more children to our table, especially those who find little recognition in their world, little to give thanks for, little to feed them. Something happens around our table, and they would be nourished there, body and soul, and maybe even changed. There are times when we invite people to our table out of a "mere" sense of hospitality. It would be rude to make sandwiches for my children on a Saturday at noon without asking their friends if they would like something as well. But if we had the opportunity to invite a child who was alone, who had no family, who had not eaten in days or weeks, to our table, we would take that opportunity not because we were afraid of being rude, but because that invitation could change or heal a life. Something happens at our table—lives are nourished, relationships are built—whether those who come there believe in lunch or not.

This is the intuition behind the emerging practice of opening the eucharistic table to all whom we can invite, whether they have been baptized or not. It's an intuition that grows from the perception that people come to our churches hungry. Hungry for community. Hungry for spirit. Hungry for love. Hungry, in other words, for God. This perception has been met by the reality of what happens at our eucharistic tables. To use Sara Miles's words, "Jesus happens" there. At our tables, Jesus is present, Jesus is in fellowship with us, and Jesus feeds us. Jesus happens at our tables regardless of the quality of our belief; and when Jesus happens, lives are changed and people are fed, sometimes to their utter surprise.

The Apostle Paul is an example of someone surprised when Jesus happened, and in that surprise his world was turned upside down. So too, in the last few decades, the church has been surprised by Jesus' happening at the eucharistic table, and again his happening is turning our world upside down. Churches are opening their eucharistic tables not out of a sense of "mere hospitality"—the simple fear of being rude. Rather, they open their tables because Jesus has happened to them there. Jesus has fed them and changed them, and at the heart of that change is the recognition that if Jesus is feeding the hungry there at the table, then we need to invite the hungry to join him. And if he is reaching out his arms in fellowship to the alienated and the lonely, then we need to invite the alienated and lonely into his embrace. And if he is giving himself at table because he so loved the world, then we need to invite the world to his table to receive that gift.

Something happens at our eucharistic tables, before and apart from our beliefs. When Jesus' story meets Jesus' presence, Jesus happens there, and we believe on account of this happening. The order is not reversed. We believe on account of Jesus happening, and what we believe is formed by Jesus happening. The church's theology begins, in many ways, there at table where Jesus' story meets his presence. The disciples on the road to Emmaus believed in resurrection because they met the living Jesus in the breaking of the bread. So it is with the emerging practice of opening our eucharistic tables to anyone we can invite.

There are some, I suppose, who issue an invitation to all simply out of a fear of being rude, but Christian communities who have reflected deeply on this practice issue a eucharistic invitation to all because of the change wrought in them at the table. The Jesus they have known at the table, the Jesus who has touched and changed their lives has turned their thinking about the Eucharist upside down.

A Robust Theology

This book began with a concern that though many Christian communities have found themselves changed through their participation at Jesus' table—converted to the practice of the open table—there was little formal theological reflection on this change and practice. In fact, the seeds for this book were planted when I heard from a theology class at the seminary where I taught that they had been assigned to debate this practice of opening the table, but those charged to argue for its legitimacy could find few resources with which to make their case.[1]

In response to the deficit, I convened a study group consisting of four parishes who practiced an open table from the Episcopal Diocese of Washington. Our work was funded by the Valparaiso Project.[2] Together we explored the meaning of this practice in our collective lives, along with its

1. An oasis in this earlier desert was Mark Stamm's *Let Every Soul Be Jesus' Guest*. His book explores the practice of opening the table largely from a Wesleyan perspective and focuses primarily on the practice and not its wider theological implications.

2. The Valparaiso Project on the Education and Formation of People in Faith is committed to funding work focused on the cultivation of religious practices in the context of Christian community. For more information, you can go to their website: www.practicingourfaith.org.

relationship to our understanding of Christian hospitality, initiation, and catechesis. Together we discovered the truth of Aidan Kavanaugh's claim that theology begins in our encounter with God through our participation in the Eucharist—that is, through our practice of hearing God's word in Scripture and gathering around Jesus' table in response.[3]

The theology that emerges from this practice of the Eucharist is inscribed on the community that participates in it. Again, from our encounter with God through God's word and at God's table we are changed, and from that change we can trace the truths of God and of our lives with which theology is concerned. Written theologies—theologies like the one I pursue in this book—come from reflection on the primary theology that God's presence inscribes on our lives.

This was the purpose of our working group—to discern how eucharistic practice inscribed a theology of the open table into the life of their communities and how the eucharistic practice of opening the table continued to shape and inform their understanding of God, church, and world, especially as this understanding was embodied in their collective life together. What emerged from our conversation was the theological centrality of God's radical grace to the eucharistic life of these communities, the intrinsic relationality of this grace, and the fundamental belief that all people who come to us are God's children. Insofar as the practice of the open table is about hospitality, it is hospitality framed in these categories.

Such a hospitality seemed to us to be simply Jesus' hospitality. This is what he practiced in his ministry—the radical grace of God embodied in the renewal of loving relationship with all of God's children, but particularly those who were neglected or outcast. This claim seemed obvious to us on the face of it—that the gospel stories were characterized throughout by this kind of hospitality—but there has been some challenge of late as to whether the word *hospitality* should apply to Jesus at all.[4] Given that Jesus spent his public ministry as an itinerant preacher (so the argument goes), that he is almost always depicted in the Gospels as a guest at a meal and not the host, does it make sense to attribute hospitality to him? Again, he was a guest at meals in the Gospels, not the host.

As I've reflected on this question, I've realized that our study group brought to all the Gospels the understanding of Jesus found in John's

---

3. Kavanaugh, *On Liturgical Theology*, 73ff.

4. See, for example, Theology Committee of the House of Bishops of the Episcopal Church, "Reflections on Holy Baptism and the Holy Eucharist."

Gospel. It's an understanding that sees in Jesus such a presence and out-pouring of grace that he is implicitly the host in any interaction. He, after all, has at his disposal the grace of the Creator. What more could any host want? Even Martha Stewart would be jealous.

I see this in John's story of the wedding at Cana, where Jesus the guest supplies for the party the best of wines, providing the other guests a bounty that the nominal hosts of the party never dreamed of. Likewise, later in the Gospel, he allows a woman at a well to "play host" to him and offer him water. He quickly turns the tables on her, though, and instructs her that if she knew with whom she was speaking, she would ask him for living water. She would recognize, in other words, his innate capacity as host. He then proceeds to give her this life.

Our study group read all of Jesus' stories through this vision of the abundant grace that fills him. It's an abundance most evident in the feeding of the 5,000—a story where Jesus' role as host is explicit and acknowledged. But in my eyes it is equally present at every meal where he gathers with tax collectors and sinners. He, after all, is the one who invited Zacchaeus to dine with him, albeit at Zacchaeus's house (Luke 19:2ff). Elsewhere, he de-scribes himself at these meals as the bridegroom who hosts wedding guests at his feast (Luke 5:34).

As we unpacked our understanding of the Eucharist and our practice of the open table, it was evident to us that our practice was bound up with our understanding of Jesus. Again, he practiced in his ministry the radi-cal grace of God embodied in the renewal of loving relationship with all of God's children. So our eucharistic theology was christological, to use the technical term. Ours was a particular Christology—a particular under-standing of Jesus. There are other ways to understand Jesus in relation to our presence and participation at his table. But from the reflections of the study group, we can't understand the meaning and reality of our practice of an open eucharistic table unless we understand it in relation to Jesus. For the group, eucharistic theology and Christology were of a piece.

In our discussion, we discovered a second truth as well—that our practice of the Eucharist engages and transforms the whole of our life to-gether through the encounter with God in Jesus that it mediates. In our conversations about the open table, we uncovered deep and deeply held beliefs about baptism, the nature of the church, and the church's mission that both inform and are informed by this practice. Indeed, the practice of the open table has only served to enrich the understanding of baptism and the importance of Christian community in the lives of these congregations, rather than diminishing them, as critics of the practice fear.

We recognized in our conversations that the life of a Christian community is integrated, especially if it is marked by any sort of intentionality and reflection. The practice of the Eucharist, the practice of baptism, an emphasis on a strong and lively Christian community—these were simply givens for the members of our study group and the parishes to which they belonged, as were the reading of Scripture, the proclamation of the gospel, the nurture of one another, and care for the world surrounding them. These practices and commitments shape the life that they share, but only as they are also held together by this shared life so that each practice shapes all the others in their mutual interaction.

Sometimes communities reflect on the relationship among these practices explicitly. All of the parishes had ongoing conversations about the relation of opening the eucharistic table to their proclamation of the gospel, for example. As often as not, the relation between practices remains implicit but active all the same. As baptism comes to seem less a ticket to heaven and more a commitment to ministry, as the Christian life comes to seem less about membership and more about service, this shapes how these communities look at their practice of the Eucharist, whether they explicitly recognize this shaping or not. Likewise, their practice of the Eucharist shapes how they understand baptism and the Christian life.

Our working group gathered to discern how eucharistic practice inscribed a theology of the open table into the life of their community. We discovered that, above and beyond any theological particulars that punctuate this practice, a theology of opening the eucharistic table is just that—a theology. It is not simply a way of looking at our practice of the Eucharist—or even less, at our desire to be hospitable and make everyone feel welcome. Rather, the theology inscribed on the hearts and minds of these communities through their encounter with Jesus at table is full and robust. It's a theology that addresses the whole of the Christian life; that's concerned with the truth of Jesus, the work of the Spirit, the significance of baptism, and the integrity and mission of the church.

An Outline

The first fruits of my work with this study group are found in an article in the *Anglican Theological Review*, "Opening the Table." The article focuses on some of the theological particulars that define this practice: that God's grace knows no boundaries and is embodied in relationships; that we all are God's children; that baptism is initiation into service, not into a club; that the church is defined by its relationship to Jesus, not by its boundaries from the world. These are core theological intuitions, if you will, that define the practice of opening our eucharistic table to all whom we can invite.

This book offers the full harvest of what was planted by our time together, developing and expanding on the core intuitions that I lay out in my article. In the pages that follow, I want to develop the theological insights that our study group discovered in two directions. I explore first the eucharistic theology of opening our tables in its relationship to an understanding of Jesus, and then I develop understandings of baptism, the work of the Spirit, and the identity and mission of the church that are interwoven with this eucharistic theology.

I begin with an investigation of how the practice of opening the table, as a eucharistic practice, is rooted in Jesus' story, or more specifically in his command that we "do this" to remember him. Luke's Gospel takes seriously this command that we understand Jesus through breaking bread at table, and so I explore how Luke brings together three strands of meal traditions in his story of Jesus' Last Supper with his disciples in order to develop an understanding of Jesus and his ministry. Jesus, I want us to see, asked us to understand him eucharistically—to understand him through his ministry at table. The insight behind the emerging practice of opening our eucharistic tables will be vital to the picture of Jesus that I develop from Luke.

This eucharistic understanding of Jesus then allows me to develop a christological understanding of the Eucharist. How, I ask in my next chapter, should we understand what we are doing at table every Sunday, given what we know about Jesus and how we have learned to understand him through his command that we "do this"? In this discussion, I explore a variety of topics: longing, thanksgiving, remembering, presence, sacrifice, covenant, eschaton, crisis, grace, and the truth of the human person. My hope, again, is to develop a broad, robust, and coherent eucharistic theology that manifests a full range of topics inherent in the Christian theological vision. The practice of the open table, I'm arguing, leads us toward this broader vision and is integral to it.

The second half of my book then turns to the broader theological intuitions and commitments bound up with this practice. In a sacramental church, what we do in our eucharistic liturgy stands in intimate relationship with what we are doing in baptism. Through the integrity of our communal life, each of these foundational practices shapes the other, so that together the two manifest a coherent theological vision.

I ground my exploration of baptism in a broad reading of the New Testament, bringing baptismal theologies from Luke-Acts, John, Mark, and Paul into conversation with one another. The understanding of baptism that emerges from this conversation centers on the essential relationship between this sacrament and the work of the Spirit—that through baptism we become loci of the Spirit's work. Given this truth, I then examine both the promises offered us by the Spirit in baptism and the demands that these promises entail. Both demands and promises are gathered in Paul's statement that in baptism, we are "clothed" in Christ (Gal 3:27); through this sacrament, we enter into the paschal mystery. When we grasp this truth, then the question of whether a practice of an open table renders baptism superfluous becomes moot. Through the Eucharist, we are brought into fellowship with Jesus, but only in baptism are we united to him. Only through baptism does Jesus' eucharistic promise come to full fruition.

A conversation that brings together baptism and the practice of opening the table is especially rich because it is the historical practice of baptism in many churches that best illuminates the faith and hope of inviting the unbaptized to the table. In the practice of infant baptism, we find the testimony *par excellence* to the church's belief that God's grace is radical and *prevenient*—that it comes first in the birth and growth of a Christian life. Moreover, in infant baptism, we find paired with this faith in God's grace a recognition that the transformation worked in baptism depends on a faithful response to grace by a person's community as well as a faithful response of the person who is baptized. Transformation into the fullness of Jesus is not magic. It is catalyzed by the fellowship with Jesus that we are offered at table and that is enacted in baptism, but it is only through the community's catechesis of love that the transformation, thus begun, comes to fruition in a Christian life.

Ultimately, the theology of Eucharist and baptism that I explore in this book are rooted in an understanding of the church that is both missional and relational. God called a church, I argue, to heal a fractured world. "All this is from God, who reconciled us to himself through Christ, and has given us the ministry of reconciliation" (2 Cor 5:18). The Christian community is a vessel of this reconciliation insofar as it is the bearer of the grace of God's embrace, of fellowship with Jesus through the practice of the Eucharist that Jesus has given us. Our baptism is baptism into this ministry.

A community defined by this ministry of restored relationship and that bears the relational grace of the Eucharist is itself relational. It is defined by the relationship of its members to one another—"Love one another as I have loved you"—but only as it is first defined by its relationship to Jesus. This for me is one of the more significant learnings that emerged from these reflections. The church that Jesus calls and constitutes through his practice of table fellowship with them is a community defined by its bonds, not its boundaries. It is our relationship with Jesus at the center of our community that makes our communities strong and gives them integrity, not the walls that separate us from the world around us. Indeed, if our primary ministry is to bear the grace of God's reconciling love to the world, one wonders what purpose such walls would serve, other than to thwart our ministry.

The church's mission and ministry, again, are to bear God's reconciling love to the world through its offer of fellowship with Jesus at his table. It is in this sense a ministry of hospitality but, again, only if hospitality is understood aright. Our hospitality is only true to Jesus if it offers the fullness of the gospel to those who come to our table hungry. It must, as well, seek to integrate those touched by the grace of Jesus' table into the full fellowship and ministry of those whose lives are centered on that table. It should, finally, be a hospitality that offers itself in service to the world, or more particularly to those whose needs are too often neglected or ignored by the world.

This is the terrain that I cover in the following pages. I explore a theology of opening the eucharistic table, but note that my emphasis is on the word "theology" in a broad sense. The practice of opening the table serves as a catalyst for this reframing of our theological maps. The purpose of the book is less to explain this one aspect of our eucharistic practice and more to explore how we might come to understand Jesus, the Spirit, the church, grace, baptism, and Eucharist through the conversation that this practice has spawned.

Scripture

I also hope that it's evident that, however much my reflections here were catalyzed by the eucharistic practice of opening the table, they are grounded in a careful and committed reading of Scripture. I read Scripture through the lens of eucharistic practice in this book, but even more I understand both this practice and the whole of the subject matter contained in these pages under the tutelage of the biblical story. Scripture provides a template for all of my explorations.

Grounding our thinking in Scripture was the consistent practice of our study group. All of our conversations were prefaced by study of a biblical text, and we tied together the conclusions of each discussion with reference to that originating text. We found that this work shaped our approach to the topic for each evening. We also found that it stretched our thinking, suggesting avenues of thought that might not have occurred to us without Scripture's guidance.

Scripture, I believe, asks to be read broadly, to be heard in the manifold ways in which it resonates with our lives. Too many forces in our world ask us to hear Scripture narrowly. For some, it is only a historical document whose chief value is to offer clues to the "real" events behind it. Once we have read off these clues, we turn from the document to the history. The document is left behind. For others, the text of Scripture is so laden with inspiration that it isn't allowed to inspire our imagination. We are asked to see a world no larger than the text, rather than seeing our world through the text.

John Calvin offered us a wonderful metaphor when he described Scripture as a pair of spectacles.[5] It is offered to help us to see the world fully and truly, to straighten and enrich our vision of the life given to us. Spectacles are given so that we might see the world—and in the case of Scripture to see the world as God's world and to see how the grace of God is incarnate in the world. We aren't true to the spectacles if we reject the world out of a devotion to the spectacles. When we do so, we've missed the point. We also have not done ourselves any favors if we ever put the spectacles aside to see the world beyond the spectacles. When we do so, the world just becomes blurry.

Scripture's spectacles help us to see the world more clearly by offering us a vision of our world. In the Gospel stories or the stories of the patriarchs, in Jesus' parables, Paul's letters, and the Psalmists' poetry, we find understandings of God and humanity in their relationship to one another played out. These stories, this poetry, these letters from Christian leaders to their communities—they explore human struggle and brokenness, the advent of grace in the midst of the struggle, and the presence and call of God that envelop the struggle.

5. Calvin, *Institutes of the Christian Religion*, I.vi.1, 69–70.

What we find throughout Scripture are living images of God in relation to God's world. In these images, we find certain characteristics, relationships, and dynamics—the fecundity of a bush, the bitterness of an older brother, or the feel of fervent love—that illuminate the characteristics, relationships, and dynamics of our world. They don't simply remind us of what we already know. They help us see the world anew. Through their lens, we are opened to realities that we didn't see before.

The Parable of the Two Sons

In this book, you will find references to a variety of scriptural stories, but you will also find one story that guides my theological exposition throughout. Jesus' parable commonly known as the Prodigal Son should perhaps be entitled the Two Lost Sons and Their Loving Father (though that isn't very pithy). This parable offers in concise form the heart of the gospel, at least as the gospel has been heard by many open-table parishes. We found in our group's discussions that we continually returned to this parable as the foundation not only for our understanding of opening the table, but for the broad array of topics that we considered.

In this way, the parable has been a catalyst for the theological visioning in the whole of this book. It contains within it an understanding of Jesus and his ministry, of the church and its mission, of the nature and working of God's grace, and of the redemption to which that grace leads us. As a parable, it conveys a vision that is both incisive and expansive. It offers the gospel in the power and breadth of its meaning, and hence it has been an invaluable resource in my thinking. Exploration of this parable will provide a useful further introduction to this book.

In the Parable of the Two Sons, a man who has left his family, wasted his inheritance, and fallen into dissolution and despair returns home seeking only lowly employment and sustenance for the most basic needs of his life. He expects to find disapproval and judgment as well. But when he arrives, he is greeted instead by the loving exuberance of his father. This father, who stood looking for the return of this alienated son since his departure, runs to meet him and, embracing him, offers him both forgiveness and a feast for which the son never dared to hope. Indeed, the father clothes him and takes him to the table before he has even had the chance to bathe.

This parable expresses concisely and eloquently Jesus' vision of God's compassionate care for humanity—a compassionate care that Jesus made incarnate in his life. It's a parable the turns on the love and forgiveness of the father, especially the fact that his forgiveness is given before it is asked for and his love seeks his son out even before he knows fully the degree to which he was lost, embracing him as soon as he is within reach.

Yes, the redemptive action of the parable is initiated by the return of the first lost son, but his return (as I discuss in the next chapter) is driven primarily by monetary concerns, the same concerns that led him to leave. The younger son in the parable is changed in the course of the story, but not by his recognition of his poverty. No, he is changed by his father—by his father's embrace, his father's invitation to the table, and by the feast and fellowship in which he is allowed, even encouraged, to share. It's clear from the father's response on his return that the father has been waiting to embrace him, and that the father's loving intention has been directed toward his son even when the son's attention was far from his father's home.

The parable, in other words, expresses a Christian intuition fundamental to our faith: that God's grace comes first (it's prevenient), and any response of love on our part is just that, a response to love that has already been offered concretely. Again, it's a response to the love that Jesus made incarnate in his life. From the perspective of communities that open their tables, this practice incarnates this expression of love to a hungry world.

There's a second side to the parable, as well, a side that queries those who have already found a seat at the father's table. For even as the father in the parable has embraced and restored his lost son, so he asks his elder son to join him at the feast. The return of his brother should be as much his concern as it is the concern of the father. But the elder son responds in anger at the father's compassion, jealous of the fellowship that he believes his father offers so carelessly.

This response reveals that there is so much that the elder son doesn't recognize. He first does not recognize that the father's fellowship is given not carelessly, but carefully, and that he himself stands within the same prevenient embrace as his brother. However faithful he has been to his father's love, his father's love came first. He was faithful to his father because of the father's embrace. He was invited to the table day by day not because he had washed, but because he was his father's son. He washed as a response to the love he received from the father and to make himself more ready to participate fully in the feast that his father had prepared. Moreover, he complains that the father never offered him a fatted calf, but he doesn't recognize that the presence of the father and fellowship with him are the essence of the feast that the father bestows. He has been the recipient of that presence and that fellowship all along.

Finally, he doesn't recognize that all that the father has is his, and that chief among these goods is the father's compassionate love for his lost children. He doesn't recognize that his service at this reconciling feast is the fruition of the inheritance of which he has been such a careful steward. The father clearly expects his son to participate in this banquet with his unwashed brother—that is the demand of his love—but this demand, from the viewpoint of the father, is itself life in his presence. It is the feast.

This Parable of the Two Sons is a parable about grace. It is a parable about grace received by the younger son and grace rejected by the elder, but only as we see its depiction of the reach of grace into our lives. The parable is adamant not only that God's grace and love come first and move us to a loving, faithful response, but also that our response of love itself is a graced privilege. All that the Father has is ours, and his chief possession, again, is his love for his children, especially those who are lost. God can bestow upon us no greater joy, no greater love than God's allowance for us to participate in God's love for our sisters and brothers. That's the grace that the elder son misses, and with it he misses life.

Why Begin Here?

We began with this parable in our study group because it named so well the grace that we experienced in our encounter with God in the Eucharist. When Jesus happened to us in this encounter, we were changed, even as the younger son was changed, and we have come to believe that the table is God's graced agent of change. It is the place of conversion through the grace of God's embrace.

As our conversation continued, though, we came to see that this parable named the grace that we experienced in the Eucharist more fully. It not only named the grace of embrace, but also the grace of service. God's embrace is also God's invitation that we join God in God's outreach to and embrace of all who seek God or who are in need of being found by God.

When we, as Christians, seek to describe our vision of God and God's world, we privilege some parts of the biblical story over others. Our vision begins someplace—with some story or text—and if the vision is coherent, it seeks to orient what we want to say about the whole of our vision around the anchor of this place. The Parable of the Two Sons served as such an anchor for our group because it articulated so fully our experience of grace not just at Jesus' table, but in the whole of the Christian life. This grace seemed an appropriate anchor for an exploration of what God is doing with us and with our world.

As I've reflected on this parable since that time, I've realized the depth of this parable more fully. The Parable of the Two Sons is not simply a rich evocation of the grace of God that we experience when Jesus happens to us; it is also an eloquent expression of the Jesus who happens. This parable is deeply christological. It speaks to the reality of Jesus, his life and his ministry, though it might be more accurate to say that Jesus in his life and ministry fulfill the gracious vision of this parable. Perhaps that's necessarily so. How can a parable speak about God's grace without finding its fulfillment in Jesus? This is why the Parable of the Two Sons serves as an anchor for me in the theology I develop in this book: because it speaks the grace fulfilled in Jesus.

What does it mean to say that this parable is fulfilled in Jesus? It means, first, that we can see Jesus in the story of the younger son. Not that he, like the younger son, has abandoned his household, but that he, in his incarnation, has joined the younger son in his alienation. That's the story that John tells in the prologue to his Gospel. He tells of how we, God's creatures, abandoned the life and light in which we were made, but that the Word, through whom we were made, became flesh and lived in our midst. He joined himself to our alienation so that he might restore us to the life that we abandoned. This is also one aspect of our understanding of Jesus' death, that in his crucifixion outside the walls of the city, we see that he has taken our sin and alienation on himself.

Jesus in his incarnation inhabits our alienation. He has joined us there where we find ourselves too often, in the far country cut off from life. He is the younger son with us, so that when we turn from our alienation to come to his table, we are not just coming to Jesus. We are also coming with Jesus. And when we receive and welcome any who come to our table, in them we are receiving and welcoming Jesus.

Jesus fulfills the role of the younger son in the parable, and he also fulfills the role of the father. He fulfills the role of the father because he is the Father's embrace for an alienated and hungry world. We hear the Father's invitation to the feast from the lips of Jesus, articulated through the whole of his life with us. When we come to Jesus' table, we receive this embrace. When we join ourselves to Jesus, we are joining ourselves to this embrace.

Jesus fulfills the role of the younger son by joining him in his alienation, and he fulfills the role of the father because he is the Father's embrace.
With the older son, though, he fulfills his place in the parable by being the
son and the brother that the elder refused to be. Jesus is the true elder son.
He is the son who understood that all that the father has is his. Thus, he
takes up the most precious of these possessions, the father's mission of love,
and he doesn't wait for the return of his lost brothers and sisters but goes
into the far country to seek them out. Finding them, he sits at table with
them and makes their meager meals into feasts, so that they might know
and be reconciled to the embrace of the Father.

The practice of the open table has been shaped as profoundly by this
latter half of the Parable of the Two Sons as it is shaped by the former half.
It is a practice that recognizes our place with the younger son, that we are
amazed and rejoice that Jesus has joined us in our alienation and that, as
the embrace of the father, he invites us to table to renew our fellowship with
him. But it's also a practice that recognizes his call to join him as a true elder
son, that we have been given the grace of sharing with him in his offer of
embrace to an alienated world.

The Christology embedded deep within the Parable of the Two Sons
makes it an ideal place to anchor a theological vision of the world. That its
Christology is centered on the grace of God embodied in the feast fits it
to the task of this book. Again, here Christology and eucharistic theology
are bound together. Our understanding of Jesus and of what happens at
table with him are intimately intertwined, and this intersection helps us to
recognize that the Eucharist is not simply a feast for the reconciled but is
rather a feast through which our reconciliation with God is catalyzed. It is
the love of the feast, the love of Jesus experienced in the feast, that opens us
to reconciliation.

The parable expresses, as well, a baptismal theology of a piece with its
eucharistic theology. It is a baptismal theology that proclaims that we are
not washed so that we might be admitted into the fellowship of the Father's
love, but that the Father's love simply showers upon us to wash us. It is a
baptismal theology that opens itself out precisely into the demand of the
gospel that we be vehicles of the Father's love and reconciliation and that we
do so not apart from the feast but precisely through our service at the feast.

In all of this, the parable expresses as well an understanding of the
church in which Christian community is defined by relationships, not by
the boundaries that demarcate who's inside or outside. The energy of the

father's love in the parable renders all boundaries ambiguous at best and perhaps even useless. The question of the parable, ultimately, is whether you accept this love and choose to participate in it, or whether you reject it and leave yourself without it. In this vision, membership in the family is the same as the ministry of the family—they both consist of living in and through the love of the Father.

A Rite, Not a Rubric

The practice of opening the table is shared among a variety of congregations across many different denominations. It is not a Methodist, Reformed, Roman Catholic, Lutheran, or Episcopal practice. It is, rather, simply the response of a large number of Christian communities to Jesus as he has happened to them in the Eucharist—in their encounter with him through word and sacrament. This book is offered to these communities and their denominations in the hope that it will enrich and deepen conversations around this practice, in part through what insights it might provide, but more importantly through whatever questions it leads others to ask.

It is likewise offered to those who have concerns about this practice across the many Christian denominations, offering them an understanding of why we might invite all to Jesus' table and what this invitation means for our understanding of Jesus, the Spirit, the church, grace, baptism, and the Eucharist. My response is shaped, in part, by questions about the relationship of this practice to the whole of the Christian life articulated by its critics, especially their questions about its relationship to baptism. There is a particular concern that offering the unbaptized an invitation to Jesus' table makes baptism superfluous—a concern that I engage in chapter 4.

Even more, my response is shaped by a critical perception that diminishes the theological and pastoral significance of this practice, and ironically, this perception is articulated as a validation of the pastoral concern behind opening the eucharistic table. Many of those skeptical of an open table agree wholeheartedly that neither clergy nor congregations are best served by taking on the role of eucharistic police, checking anyone who approaches the altar for baptismal papers. They also often agree that there are certain "pastorally sensitive" situations, such as a wedding or funeral, where we are likely to have unbaptized persons in our midst whom we would like to participate fully in the joy or comfort offered in our liturgy. Their concern about an open table, they want to be clear, is more about a fundamental policy of inviting all to the table, regardless of baptismal status, and less about particular applications of eucharistic restriction or nonrestriction.

While these avowals do exhibit a commendable pastoral concern, they nonetheless serve to reduce the practice of opening Jesus' table to a mere rubric in our eucharistic practice. Rubrics are the italicized footnotes that accompany the written forms of our liturgy, reminding us of what is allowed, permitted, or forbidden in a worship service. So we are told that here we might stand or that there we can hug or shake hands when we share Jesus' peace.

Treating an open table as a practice of "pastoral sensitivity" relegates it to a simple instruction allowing broader participation in the Eucharist in certain instances, while denying it any deeper theological or evangelical sense. "Yes, we want to take care that we don't offend individuals in delicate situations, but that has nothing to do with unloosing the love and grace of Jesus to heal and change a broken world."

If opening the eucharistic table, inviting all present to participate in fellowship with Jesus, isn't a mere rubric—an instruction that we offer simply to smooth out our gatherings for worship—then what is it? Aidan Kavanaugh offers us a different approach to this practice that is more true to the theological significance that it manifests in communities that have embraced it. It is an approach that comes out of his exploration of liturgical acts and rites.[6]

Liturgical acts are those many different things that we do in our gathering for worship—the reading of the Gospel, the sharing of the prayers of all the people, the celebration of a feast at Jesus' table. Kavanaugh wants us to see that these acts are not atomized functions that have been haphazardly gathered to make up a service. Rather, they are the place where our worship of God and our beliefs about God converge. They are intentional, they stand in intimate relation to one another, and together they exhibit a synergy that makes up a larger whole. This larger whole Kavanaugh labels a rite, and by rite he doesn't simply mean a customary style of worship but rather, as he puts it, "a whole style of Christian living."[7]

The whole of our worship or liturgy catches up the deepest truths that we seek to embody in our Christian lives. The various actions that make

6. Kavanaugh, *On Liturgical Theology*, 100ff.
7. Ibid.

up our worship stand in intimate relation to this whole. They are concrete embodiments of this whole.

This is what it means to say that the practice of opening the table is a rite and not a rubric. It is to say that it is not simply an occasional means of accommodating certain pastoral concerns, but rather it is an articulation of the Christian community's response to God's grace. It is a part of a whole response, it can be understood only in relationship to that whole, and it speaks to the truth of that whole if we will only listen.

This book is an attempt to lay out at least one vision of the rite—the whole style of Christian living—of which the practice of an open table is a part. Again, this is why this book is as much about understanding Jesus, the Spirit, the church, grace, and baptism as it is about eucharistic practice per se. The practice of the open table exists within a style of Christian living that believes deeply in the gracious power of Jesus' presence at table, the work of the Spirit to integrate us into the paschal mystery that we encounter at the table, and the call of the church to live out this mystery in the world.

For Kavanaugh, the rites to which our liturgical acts are tied are whole styles of Christian living. Conversely, the liturgical acts within a rite are the way "a redeemed world is done." Again, they are concrete expressions of the grace that Christian communities have received from God and the response of these communities to that grace. We call this the "doing of re-demption," not because we have taken the task of redemption away from God, but because God has graciously invited us to participate in God's work through Jesus and the Spirit.

Looking back to the beginning of this series of introductions, when the church celebrates the eucharistic meal, Jesus happens, revealing and making present the bread of life for which the world is hungry. We open our tables on the basis of our commitment to the reality of what happens here and to our belief that the world is truly hungry for this happening. We feed Jesus to all who would come to him not as a mere act of hospitality, but as a redemptive act of hospitality. We believe that those who have tasted and seen that the Lord is good will be moved to join themselves to him and to the body through which he manifests and enacts this goodness in the world.

The recognition that opening the table is a rite and not a rubric, that it is a whole style of Christian living through which the redeemed world is done and not merely a simple invitation that we offer on Sunday morning, is important for critics of this practice to understand. Even more, it is the great challenge of this practice to those communities that have embraced it.

There is something peaceful and warm for many congregations about extending a welcome to everyone present to participate in the eucharistic meal; we are glad that no one is left out. But on my reading of this practice, we have only truly grasped its implications when we recognize the power of what we do in this invitation and when we struggle to embody this powerful deed in the whole of our ecclesial life. The table that we open is a table where Jesus happens. It is a table where God is present through our fellowship with the crucified carpenter whose invitation we are answering. We can only open our table in good faith to those on the outside if we are honest with them and with ourselves about the profound thing that happens there.

Opening the table, moreover, challenges us to take baptism seriously as a commitment to the way of Christ's mission to all of us who are lost. This means not only that those within the church need to embrace their baptism and the grace of this mission that it offers. It means also that we must steadfastly encourage baptism for those who come to our table seeking Jesus, that they may not only be found by him but be united to him with us.[8]

It challenges us to take hospitality seriously, for it means little to open our eucharistic table if we don't also open the tables in our parish halls and homes. So too, opening the table challenges us to take service to the world seriously. How can we claim that Christ's outreach to the outcast and oppressed justifies the opening of our tables if we don't, with the same energy and commitment, reach out to the outcast and oppressed in our world?

This recognition that opening the table is a whole style of Christian living stands as a rejoinder to those who reject this practice as a capitulation of the church to a comfortable, worldly hospitality. It is hospitality that

---

8. There is obviously a tension here between two movements within the church that have led to the practice of opening the table. On the one hand, we open the table to the seeker who comes to our churches, seeking God but not knowing what this means. Through the invitation to come and dine with Christ, we communicate something of the love of God that has found us in Christ. At the same time, many congregations are opening their tables to those of diverse faith traditions within their midst—Jewish, Muslim, or Buddhist spouses, for example. Intrinsic to this move is a concern to express a respect for the religious commitments of all invited guests. This first and primary dynamic of opening the table that I mention here necessitates that it be accompanied by an invitation to know Christ and to be joined with him in baptism. But the second dynamic sits uncomfortably with this reality. I will struggle with this tension in a later chapter.

takes quite seriously the church's intimate relationship with the world, but it is hardly comfortable. This recognition stands as such a rejoinder, however, only as it functions fully and clearly in our understanding and practice of the open table. Indeed, the challenge for the churches who open their tables is not to justify this practice but to fulfill it, to embody in their whole lives the grace, compassion, and active care for the world that they enact in this opening.

CHAPTER 2

Jesus and the Table

If only Jesus Christ is holy, then holiness itself confutes our expectation. The image of Jesus in the New Testament discloses one who did not protect his ritual purity, who freely gave away his holy separation, who criticized the ritual gift to God. Moreover, his death was itself deeply foul and unclean, a participation in the lot of slaves and rebels. . . . If only Jesus Christ is holy, then God's holiness is the very giving away of holiness to others, for others.

—GORDON LATHROP, *HOLY THINGS*

"Do THIS FOR THE remembrance of me." All four Gospels along with Paul recount that Jesus shared a meal with his closest disciples on the night before his death. They explain that in this meal he anticipated his death and prepared his disciples for it, and they agree that this preparation included a promise of his presence after his death.[1] Luke, Mark, and Matthew, along with Paul, relate that Jesus blessed and shared bread and a cup of wine with his friends that night, asking them to understand this sharing in its relation to his giving himself to bring about God's kingdom. Luke, along with Paul, captures the sense of this action when he tells us that Christ commanded his disciples to do this—to take, bless, break, and share the bread, to bless and share the cup: to remember him. Much of this—that Jesus shared a meal with his disciples, prepared them for his death, and intended them to

---

1. In Paul and the Synoptic Gospels, this presence is promised through their continued table fellowship with Jesus. In John, it is promised by the coming of the Comforter.

keep alive this preparation in their shared table fellowship—I would hold to be historically probable.

Jesus, these accounts agree, taught the disciples that night how to do Christology. (Christology is the theological term for how we think and talk about Jesus, about who he was and what he did.) He taught them how to understand him, how to remember him, and in our discussion of this short command, we must always be mindful that the Greek word "remember"—*anamnesis*—means so much more than merely to call to mind. When Israel was to remember God in their celebration of the Passover, they weren't simply to recollect that God once saved them. Theological remembering is about more than a memory, distant and wistful. It's about presence. Not the calling of another into our presence—it's not magic. Rather, at least for Israel at Passover and for the disciples who remember Jesus, it is to place oneself in the presence of the Holy Other and to know with one's heart the weight of that presence. It is to enter relationship in an immediate and intimate way. What is closer to our hearts than our memory? That night, Jesus taught the disciples how to remember him, how to know him, and in this he taught them how to do Christology.

That's the supposition of this theology—that this action, where in our remembering we are present to Jesus, is essential to knowing and understanding Jesus. That's the lesson we gain from the disciples on the road to Emmaus—that we know Jesus in the breaking of the bread. In part, this is a recognition of the centrality of our experience. We know Jesus through this experience. But it is also a statement about our intellectual grappling with Jesus. To know Jesus is more than to recognize his presence. It is to bring the whole of his story to that presence. It is to remember someone with a history that defines who he is. So when Jesus tells us to do *this* to remember him, he is telling us something about our recollection of his story in its relation to his presence with us at the table. In doing *this*, we remember *him*, not some other, and we remember him by remembering his story.

Gordon Lathrop has reminded us that our liturgies multiply, enrich, and add nuance to meaning through acts of juxtaposition.[2] In our worship, we hold together word and sacrament, supplication and praise, cross and resurrection; and when we do so, each draws from the other a fecundity of meaning through their mutual interaction. The cross becomes a symbol of life, while resurrection is colored with the full pathos of human existence. Jesus, according to the Gospels, juxtaposes this action—the blessing,

2. Lathrop, *Holy Things*, 15–24, 79ff.

breaking, and sharing at the table—with the whole of his story. We are to do this to remember his story and to do it while remembering his story. We cannot understand what we do apart from that story, and we understand that story by doing this. Each becomes the lens through which we refract the other.

In our next chapter, I will ask the question of how our understanding of Jesus in the whole of his story shapes our understanding and practice of this action that he told us to do. I'll ask how Jesus shapes our understanding of the Eucharist. That's the question of how Christology affects our practice of liturgy. But in this chapter, I first need to ask the other question—how Jesus' command to do this shapes our understanding of the whole of his story. In this command, Jesus told us how to do Christology. We do *this* to remember him. So I now will move from Jesus' liturgy—his breaking of the bread with his disciples—to Christology: how this blessing, gift, and fellowship shape our understanding of his story as a whole.

Indeed, this command is significant for our task precisely because of the power of this practice to focus and shape the story through which we remember Jesus. The stories or narratives in which we live shape our lives. In a general way, they form the backdrop to the living of our lives. The stories that circulate within a culture provide values, goals, and virtues that shape the characters and decisions of those who live within them.

More specifically, each of us has a narrative or array of narratives residing within us that forms our sense of our own story. As we make decisions, as we respond to events, in those moments when we have the opportunity to reflect on our actions, we tend to act not simply in response to the particulars of a situation, but also with an eye to the larger story of ourselves that we are crafting through that response. We inhabit our own stories, so that we serve both as the lead actor and, to some degree, the author of that story—our actions are governed in many ways by that authority, whether the authoring self and his or her story resides at a conscious or unconscious level.

The stories by which we remember someone else, then, cut closest to the heart of that person when they are guided by some insight into the narrative or narratives by which that person lived his or her life. We understand someone best when we can intimate the story that they told themselves as they moved through their lives. Yet access to these narratives is hindered by the inherent ambiguity of the storied character of any actual life.

Although some are able to exercise a mature integration of their lives into a more or less consistent story, the haphazard character of actual life makes this difficult for most. Consider: we play minor roles in countless other narratives authored by everyone with whom we come in contact. We have little or no control over the broader events that form the backdrop to and impinge upon our stories. We must constantly make narrative choices with little or no time for reflection. This haphazard character of our lives allows even the more integrated lived narratives little of the consistency and possible indications of authorial intent that mark literary narratives, and literary narratives (novels or shorts stories) can serve as simplified models for the lived narratives that we are now considering.[3] In fact, even literary narratives are ambiguous. That's why they employ innumerable faculty in innumerable departments of literature who work to discern their substance and end. Nonetheless, these narratives are able through their structure and content to guide their readers along pathways that form at least a limited arena for debate. Lived narratives are seldom able to employ these effects.

If we take seriously Jesus' humanity, then we must assume that some narrative or narratives guided his actions. Indeed, a strand of christological discussion of the past two centuries—and especially the project of the "search" for the historical Jesus—has been concerned to unearth these narratives, asking questions about how Jesus thought of himself. For example, some have asked whether Jesus was writing with his life the story of the Messiah as he made the decisions that directed his steps, or was his self-understanding shaped more by the story of a prophet or a Near Eastern sage?[4]

In the four Gospels, we find the claim that we have some insight into Jesus' narrative understanding of his life through his last meal with his disciples—that he understood his situation, and so he prepared his disciples, in the face of his impending death, to grasp his life through the practice of this shared meal. This final meal was to provide for them some clue to the substance and end of his story as he understood it, so that his story, formed around this clue, could serve as a remembered narrative that might

---

3. Paul Ricoeur recounts with eloquence the ambiguities that assault lived narratives, to the degree that the category of narrative is questionable when applied to manifold events and occurrences of our lives. See Ricoeur, *Oneself As Another*, 159–61.

4. See William Wrede, *The Messianic Secret*, for a seminal denial of Jesus' messianic consciousness. So in John Crossan's work, we find a claim for Jesus as a "peasant Jewish Cynic," while in the work of Marcus Borg, he is depicted as a Near-Eastern sage. See Crossan, *The Historical Jesus*, 422, and Borg, *Meeting Jesus Again for the First Time*, 69–95.

continue to shape their lives. They were to do it, as Luke recalls, to remember him, and in remembering him to be shaped by him.

To accept this claim of the Gospels, we need not accept their crafted narration of this final meal as a verbatim report of the clue that Jesus was giving. The Gospel accounts of Jesus' last meal evidence the reflection of countless Christian communities emerging from their own practice of Jesus' meal. The practice of these communities renders these accounts into a liturgical whole. The words recorded in the Gospels have the shape of a liturgy, and we can doubt that Jesus authored such a well-formed liturgy that night as he faced his death.[5] These accounts are, nonetheless, central to our remembering of Jesus if we can accept that their narration points us back to the historically probable event of a shared meal of preparation for Jesus' death where he offered his disciples a clue to the meaning of his life.

The leap we must make, then, is that their interpretation of this clue in their own narratives—their accounts of the Last Supper—are accurate to the meal hosted by Jesus that night. We must accept that the story of Jesus taking, blessing, breaking, and sharing bread and blessing and sharing a cup while relating both of these acts to his act of giving himself captures the understanding of his story that Jesus conveyed to his disciples.

If we make this leap, we are not imposing a monolithic interpretation on the narrative of Jesus' life. It's evident simply from the divergent accounts of this final meal in the four Gospels that Jesus' narrative clue could be interpreted in a multitude of ways. Indeed, John interprets it through a story that focuses on foot washing, not the blessing and distribution of bread and a cup.

Rather, if we decide to work with the Gospel accounts of Jesus' Last Supper, we are simply claiming that a reading of Jesus' own story through the lens of the command to do this to remember him is not only attentive to the integrity of Jesus' story but should offer us real insight into that story. Reading the story of Jesus through the practice of the Eucharist, in other words, is not a foreign imposition on that story by the church but is an organic development of that story as Jesus offered it to his disciples.

In this book, I will accept the Gospel accounts of Jesus' last meal with his disciples as a faithful interpretation of Jesus' actions and intentions that night. I do this in part because I find them the most historically credible

5. Bradshaw makes a convincing case that Jesus' words of institution repeated in the Synoptic Gospels originated not as liturgical texts or instructions to guide the celebration of the early Christian Eucharist, but as a "catechesis of a liturgical kind," explaining the beliefs implicit in their celebration. See Bradshaw, *Eucharistic Origins*, 14–21.

witnesses to Jesus and his story, though I must admit that all of our witnesses to this story stand at such a chronological distance from the story that their testimony can bear very little historical weight. I am not claiming, in other words, to have found the true historical Jesus, given the historical emptiness of that project.[6] Rather, I am following the Gospel witness because I find it credible and, more importantly, because I have chosen to make the biblical authors my companions.[7] I have chosen to accept their account of Jesus' story because I believe that I share that story with them.

This companionship can mean many things, but for our discussion it means that I, with them, have found Jesus present in and recognized Jesus through the breaking of the bread. It means that this practice has refracted Jesus' story for me in a manner that rings true to God and life as I have come to know them. And I am not alone in this companionship—I share it with countless millions Christians from the past two millennia who have shared this story and practice as well. It may seem circular for me to accept a witness to a history as true because I have experienced the truth of the witness's construal of the history, but there is a certain circularity to the process of knowing most things.[8] We always read history and our own experience of reality together, so that what we know of each informs our understanding of the other. The liturgical/scriptural Christology that will center this book is such a reading of history and reality together, arguing that they intersect precisely in the practice of the breaking of the bread as narrated in the Gospels.

The Breaking of the Bread

Given this decision to read Jesus' story through the lens of the breaking of bread at his Last Supper with his disciples, we will allow Luke's account of Jesus' story to guide us in our understanding of Jesus, though we will not limit ourselves to Luke's testimony. Luke's is the Gospel that asks us to do this to remember Jesus, and it is, more importantly, the Gospel that situates

6. See Johnson, *The Real Jesus*, especially 81–104.

7. For more on this idea of companionship, see Greene-McCreight, "'We Are Companions of the Patriarchs.'"

8. John Dominic Crossan makes a very similar point to this. See Crossan, *The Historical Jesus*, 422ff. It's fascinating, though, to read Marcus Borg's sharp distinctions between the historical Jesus and the Christ of faith, given his testimony to the coherence of the Christ that he found in faith to his reconstruction of the historical Jesus. See Borg, *Meeting Jesus Again for the First Time*, 1–19.

the fourfold action of the breaking of the bread (taking, blessing, breaking, and giving) as the interpretive center of his story.

Luke, in other words, understood systematically the command to do this to remember Jesus, and so he organized his memory of Jesus precisely around this practice. In Luke's Gospel, we find Jesus taking, blessing, breaking, and giving bread not only at the Last Supper but also at the feeding of the 5,000, after which he turns from his ministry in Galilee to head toward Jerusalem and the cross, and with the two disciples on the road to Emmaus, where he reveals both the meaning of his death and ministry and the truth of his resurrection. By placing Jesus' breaking of the bread at the three nodal points in his narrative—Jesus' culmination of his Galilean ministry, his embrace of the cross, and his revelation of himself in his resurrection—Luke is demanding that we understand Jesus through this action, and so we will acquiesce to that demand. But what, exactly, is Jesus commanding his disciples to do?

Luke's detailed specificity about Jesus' taking, blessing, breaking, and giving the bread, together with his use of this action to bind together the events of the feeding of the 5,000, Jesus' Last Supper, and the meal at Emmaus, highlights the importance of this detailed action as the substance of Jesus' command. It will, in many ways, bear the fecundity of the meaning of this meal that Luke wants to convey to us. But we will get a handle on this surplus of meaning if we can ask first more broadly about what Jesus has commanded his disciples to do—if we can ask, that is, about the context for this command to take, bless, break, and share the bread.

If in Luke Jesus institutes at his Last Supper with his disciples a remembrance of himself, then the first celebration of this remembrance would be at the inn at Emmaus after Jesus' resurrection. There Jesus blesses and breaks the bread with his two disciples at the table. In this story, we find alongside the repetition of the fourfold action the accompanying emphasis on table fellowship. When the two disciples return and report their encounter with the risen Christ, they say that they knew him "in the breaking of the bread," a generic description of the fourfold action that points us as much to the context of the breaking—the table fellowship that it consecrates—as it does to this action itself.

This phrase is repeated throughout Luke's account of the early church, most notably in Acts 2:42, where we're told that the first Christians continued in the apostles' teaching, the fellowship, and the breaking of the bread. "The breaking of the bread" in these stories serves as a bridge concept, holding together the fourfold action of Jesus with the broader idea of table fellowship to which it is tied.

Table fellowship here refers not simply to sharing a meal with another, but to the formation of community around a shared meal consciously held in the presence of God—the bread that is broken is always bread that has first been blessed and then shared with a community of blessing around the table. So when Jesus commands his disciples to do this—to take, bless, break, and give the bread to one another—he is commanding them to continue in the table fellowship that he shared with them that night before his death, and in that fellowship to remember him. That they understood this command is evident in our reports of their community throughout Acts.

We can begin to understand how the command to do this to remember Jesus shapes our understanding of him by first exploring what this theme of table fellowship brings to Luke's story. Luke's Gospel is a gospel of table fellowship.[9] It is not only oriented around the three meals in which Jesus is said explicitly to perform the fourfold action of taking, blessing, breaking, and giving bread at table, but it is also permeated with stories of meals, and stories of stories of meals.

We can understand Luke only if we understand at least some of what he says through these many accounts of Jesus' meals and parables about meals. Jesus' last meal with his disciples is one such meal within Luke's account, but it is clearly also centrally situated within the narrative to draw together the many strands of the meal traditions in Luke. For our purposes, it will be worthwhile to identify three of these strands and then to explore them in detail.

Luke, in the first place, draws our attention strongly to Jesus' Last Supper with his disciples as a Passover meal, an understanding that he shares with both Mark and Matthew. A contemporary debate rages about the historical likelihood that this last meal was a Passover meal, but any definitive answer to this question will elude us. Not only do we lack sufficient agreement among the Christian witnesses to Jesus' meal to construct a convincing historical account, but we also lack sufficient Jewish witness to the first-century practice of Passover to provide us with the necessary context through which we could reconstruct Jesus' last meal.[10]

---

9. This was suggested by Karris, *Luke,* 47–78.

10. See Johnson, *The Gospel of Luke,* 340–41, for a brief but effective discussion of this issue.

This lack of historical clarity does not, however, cloud the literary clarity of Luke's interpretation of Jesus' last meal with his disciples as a Passover meal. He narrates both that Jesus ordered the disciples to prepare a Passover meal that they might share together, and that Jesus explains his desire to share this Passover with his disciples at the beginning of the meal. For Luke, we cannot understand Jesus' command to break and share this bread at table together apart from the Passover tradition in which he situates it.

Within the Christian tradition that follows Luke and the other Synoptic Gospels, the paschal understanding of Jesus' last meal was essential to their understanding of his death. Jesus, dying at the time of the Passover (of this we are largely certain), was seen as the Passover lamb who gave his life to deliver his people from their slavery to sin and death. The early church's growing awareness of this understanding after Jesus' death is signaled in Luke's Gospel by Christ's instruction of the disciples on the road to Emmaus—only then, after his death, do they begin to understand the significance of his death. But Luke also roots this understanding in Jesus' instruction of his disciples at this last meal—again, as he takes, blesses, breaks, and shares the bread of the meal with them, instructing them that the bread is his body, given for them. This instruction, occurring at a Passover meal, would point the disciples to a paschal interpretation of Christ's death as his gift of his body for their salvation.

Again, we cannot know what Jesus said at this final meal with his disciples, nor whether it was even a Passover meal. But it is difficult to imagine that Jesus would prepare his disciples for his death, while ignoring the great feast of the Passover that surrounded them. Jesus would lose all credibility as a great preacher if he were to ignore such a teachable moment. A strong argument can be made, moreover, for at least the minimal claim that at this meal, Jesus did break and offer his disciples the bread, referring it to his gift of himself.[11] Thus, whether this last meal was a Passover seder or not, we can accept Luke's account of a paschal context for this meal as a faithful interpretation of it. Jesus' command to continue in the breaking of the bread in order to remember and understand him, then, needs to be understood in light of what it says about his life and death as a paschal mystery.

Much of the eucharistic theology that surrounds the church's understanding of Christ's Last Supper with his disciples is oriented around this paschal context to the meal. This theology thus orients our understanding of Christ's last meal in relation to his imminent death on the cross—the

11. See Leon-Dufour, *Sharing the Eucharistic Bread,* 46–94, especially 84ff.

meal standing as our interpretation of and participation in that death. This cruciform theology of Jesus' last meal and of his command to break bread at table to remember him will also bear much weight in our understanding of Jesus, but we must take care not to allow it to overshadow the other meal traditions that Luke invokes in his account of Christ's history. We cannot allow them to be occluded in our account of Christ's story. We have not fully remembered or understood Jesus if we isolate his cross from his ministry or his resurrection, to which these other traditions point us.

Luke has Jesus explicitly invoke one of these traditions—the tradition of the messianic banquet, the eschatological feast celebrated at the fulfillment of God's kingdom—as he begins this last meal with the disciples. "For I tell you, I shall not eat [this Passover again] until the time when it is fulfilled in the kingdom of God" (Luke 22:16). "I will certainly not drink the fruit of the vine from now until the kingdom of God comes" (Luke 22:18).

A hope for God's kingdom is explicit within the tradition of the Passover meal—a meal that recalls God's salvation of God's people in the past as a promise of God's future deliverance. But Jesus' references to the coming of God's kingdom here at his last Passover also invokes the theme of the coming kingdom that not only overarched his ministry as a whole but also came to particular expression in parables of the messianic kingdom feast. After teaching his disciples repeatedly that the kingdom of God is like a feast, he now informs them that this kingdom feast lay imminently before him. (Note the word "eschatological" in the previous paragraph. It's a theological term that refers to the end of times when God breaks into history and redeems it. The term "messianic" in connection to this reminds us of God's chosen one who inaugurates this in-breaking of God's kingdom.)

Echoes of this teaching about the kingdom feast reverberate through the early church's celebration of the table fellowship to which they were directed by Jesus. The breaking of bread at Emmaus would stand as the first such feast, when the resurrected Jesus reveals himself in intimacy to his disciples. The meals reported in Acts also stand in the tradition of this Emmaus meal, often invoking not the paschal themes referred to above, but rather resonating with the joy of gathering in the presence of the risen Christ, praising God for the victory of Easter.[12] We see this eschatological tradition carried on in the table liturgies of the early Christian community, most notably the Didache.[13]

12. Leon-Dufour compares them with the Jewish *todah* meals. See ibid., 39ff.

13. See Bradshaw, *Eucharistic Origins*, 36–37, for a discussion of the eschatological

Jesus' proclamation that he would share this meal again only with the fulfillment of the kingdom carries with it a studied ambiguity, pointing back to his parables of the messianic feast while pointing forward to his presence with those who share in fellowship in remembrance of him. Thus, alongside the cruciform witness of the paschal tradition to Jesus' last meal, we must also hold the eschatological witness to Jesus' resurrection and the messianic feast invoked in Luke's account.

We will fully grasp what Jesus is telling us about himself, however—the clue that he is offering us for the interpretation of his life—if we understand his breaking of bread with his disciples at this last meal in connection to the countless times that he broke bread with disciples, with followers, with onlookers, and even with opponents throughout his ministry. When Jesus commanded his disciples to break bread together to remember him, he was not commanding an utterly new practice; he was asking them to take up what had been utterly common, and at the same time utterly remarkable, about their life together, and to take it up explicitly as a way to remember and make him present.[14]

Both traditional and progressive readers of Jesus' story have resisted holding together the Gospel reports of Jesus' last meal with the meals that fill the rest of their accounts. Some involved in the new search for the Jesus of history want to dismiss any last meal of Jesus in which he prepares his disciples for what comes ahead, choosing to understand him only through the practice of table fellowship that they find described in accounts of his wider ministry. As I suggest in the introduction to this chapter, I find it highly unlikely that Jesus did not anticipate his death, given that he deliberately marched to Jerusalem to confront authorities who had never hesitated to put their opponents to death. It is also unlikely that Jesus wouldn't prepare his disciples for these final events when they were at table together. I have chosen to take the accounts of this preparation offered in the canonical Gospels as faithful to Jesus' final meal of preparation.

Some of those who support inviting only the baptized to the eucharistic table have likewise advocated understanding Jesus' last meal apart from the rest of his meals narrated in the Gospels, arguing that this meal

---

orientation of the table liturgy in the Didache.

14. So Dix argues that Jesus' command to his disciples was not so much to do this— the this was a table fellowship that they almost certainly would repeat—but to do it to remember him. The remembering is the key element of the command. See Dix, *The Shape of the Liturgy*, 55.

is special and distinct—one meant for only the closest of his followers.[15] This argument is also lacking. It begins from a specious premise—that this last meal of Jesus with one who would betray him to death, with one who would deny him explicitly, with many who would abandon him, and with all who did not understand him well enough to truly believe in him—that the gathering at this last meal of Jesus was in some way distinct from the gathering of his previous meals. One could argue that however inauspicious his guests were at this last meal, they formed a distinct company of those chosen and loved by Jesus, but this argument would have to maintain that these disciples were more chosen and loved by Jesus than were the poor, oppressed, and outcast with whom he dined earlier in his ministry.

More importantly, this argument ignores the explicit connection made by Luke (and found, as well, in Matthew and Mark) tying this meal to Jesus' table fellowship in his Galilean ministry. Luke, as we have seen, draws a distinct parallel between this meal, which culminates Jesus' march to the cross, and his feeding of the 5,000, which culminates Jesus' ministry of table fellowship with Pharisees, followers, tax collectors, and sinners throughout his Galilean ministry. In both places, Jesus gathers a motley group, blesses, breaks, and shares bread, and offers himself to those gathered through this ministry.

For Luke's Gospel, we can understand Jesus' command to bless, break, and share bread at table in remembrance of him and his gift of himself only if we see this act in the context of Jesus' wider practice of table fellowship that was so definitive of his ministry. This is not to dismiss the paschal or eschatological themes that Luke's account also invokes. It is, rather, to argue that we must hold these three together and understand them in their relationship to one another, much as Luke has done, by tying together the feeding of the 5,000, the Last Supper, and the resurrection meal at Emmaus through the repetition of the fourfold action.

In many ways, this is obvious. All I am saying is that we must understand Jesus' ministry, death, and resurrection together as guided by the breaking of bread that he commanded at his Last Supper. Too often, however, Christian retellings of Jesus' story have placed so much emphasis on the cross that his ministry is entirely obscured. This is the mistake that we are trying to avoid, under Luke's guidance. Again, not that we will ignore the cross, but we will see it in its full significance only as we allow it to

---

15. See, for example, Farwell, "Baptism, Eucharist, and the Hospitality of Jesus," 220ff.

illuminate and be illuminated by its relationship to Christ's ministry as the narrative context in which it occurs.

If we are to follow the narrative clue that Jesus gives us at his last meal with his disciples and allow the breaking of bread to shape our telling of Jesus' story, then we must tell that story with an eye to the paschal, eschatological, and ministerial themes that inform it. We will begin to do this by looking first at Jesus' ministry through the lens of his practice of table fellowship. We will then explore how Jesus' teaching about the kingdom feast expands what we have seen about Jesus' table fellowship and its culmination in his Last Supper. Finally, we will come back to the paschal themes that Luke highlights so clearly around this meal, and then to the specifics of the fourfold action as a way of holding all of this together.

Table Fellowship

Luke's Gospel, as I said above, is a story of table fellowship. Throughout the Gospel, scholars have commented, Jesus is either at a meal, going to a meal, or coming from a meal.[16] For Luke, you cannot properly remember Jesus apart from these meals and what he says about them. We must understand, however, that these meals are not simply about food but about fellowship; hence, the emphasis on table fellowship. It's not that food isn't important in these stories of meals—what makes a shared meal significant in the first place is the sharing and consumption of the stuff of life. We don't, for example, understand the story of the feeding of the 5,000 at all if we don't get that Jesus feeds a hungry multitude. Food, in this story, is the gift, while also serving as a metaphor for God's greater gift. We don't live by bread alone, but we don't live without bread, either.

Food is significant in relationship to these stories of meals not only as that which nourishes our bodies but also as that around which we gather our communities. We build our social relationships through food and the offer of food, and life depends upon these relationships as much as it depends on the food that we are offered through them. Food is significant, then, for the fellowship that it constitutes.

Within the context of the biblical story, there is a holiness to food as the stuff of life given to us by God, and this holiness sanctifies the relationships through which food is shared and consumed. This holiness is evident in the mandate of hospitality. Abraham shares food with three travelers and

16. Karris, *Luke*, 47–78.

entertains angels unawares. He establishes relationship with these strangers through his offer of food, while God establishes relationship with him likewise through his hospitality. Through his offer of food, Abraham has fellowship with God. (This insight is captured beautifully in Rublev's icon of the Trinity.)

Anthropologists have long noted the capacity for the sharing of food to define social relationships. To know who shares food with whom in a society is to have a social map of that society, insofar as this sharing of food initiates "an interconnected complex of mutuality and reciprocity."[17]

In Jesus' Jewish milieu, this capacity of food sharing to define social relationships was heightened by its theological dimension. Jewish meals always begin with a blessing, the *berakah*—"Blessed be thou, O Lord our God, eternal King, who bringest forth bread from the earth." This divine invocation acknowledges that the web of relationship that the meal enacts is always already grounded in the relationship of the participants to God who provides the meal, who is the ultimate host. Thus, Gillian Feeley-Harnik argues that every Jewish meal is in some sense a covenant meal—a meal of the community who have bound themselves to one another through their mutual belonging to or being fed by God.[18] This covenantal sense of the meal was strengthened in the years following the Babylonian captivity of the Jews, when a heightened awareness emerges of the power of purity laws surrounding their food to bind the Jewish people to one another, to mark them off as God's people in the midst of their enemies.

Meals, then, in Jesus' Jewish context were occasions for establishing and celebrating both the boundaries around and the relationships among God's people, as distinct from those outside of God's covenant—those who were impure, apostate, or who worshiped false gods. To break bread with another—and we must remember that blessing the bread was intrinsic to its breaking—was to proclaim God and to claim, with the other, fellowship with God through that action.

We can understand the Gospel accounts of Jesus' meal ministry and what they tell us of Jesus only when we grasp this theological dimension to these meals. Some contemporary scholars have emphasized the social revolution that Jesus initiated through his willingness to eat with the outsiders; he subverted the class system, they claim, through which the powerful

---

17. Klosinski, *The Meals in Mark*, 56–58. See also Farb and Armelagos, *Consuming Passions*, 4, 211. Taken from Crossan, *The Historical Jesus*, 68-69.

18. Feeley-Harnik, *The Lord's Table*, 71–106.

ordered society, and so he was a threat to the system and the power that it maintained.[19] What the analysis misses is the dependence of this social revolution on an underlying religious revolution—that Jesus, in his meal ministry, challenged contemporary understandings of both the makeup of the people of God (those with whom God was in fellowship) and God's approach to those who stood outside this fellowship. Again, to break bread with someone in Jesus' context was to share fellowship with God.

Jesus' meal ministry, to return to the previous chapter, needs to be understood through the lens of the Parable of the Prodigal Son. Certainly we understand the parable only as we see the shift in the relationship between the two brothers—a social revolution of a kind—but it's clear within the parable that this shift is driven by the revolution in relationship that needs to take place between each brother and the father. Indeed, if we read the parable with Jesus taking the part of the father, it is remarkable the insight that it offers to Jesus' meal ministry overall. In his meals with the tax collectors and sinners, we see the father's reception of the prodigal younger brother who returns to his father's house and embrace. In his meals with the religious authorities, we see the father's instruction of the elder brother regarding his misunderstanding of his relationship with both his father and the prodigal.

In both cases, Jesus is seeking to reconcile God's lost children to the ways and fellowship of the Father. Indeed, we could argue that Jesus' practice of table fellowship was his own liturgy of reconciliation. This will be clearer if we look at his table fellowship in relation not only to the tax collectors and sinners and to the religious authorities, but also to his disciples, always with the template of the Parable of the Prodigal to guide us. Once we are clear on the dynamics of this table fellowship, we can turn to Jesus' eschatological teaching on this fellowship to develop more fully the theological dimension of Jesus' liturgy of reconciliation.

Jesus and the Younger Son

Perhaps the most notable and historically reliable aspect of Jesus' ministry was his table fellowship with tax collectors and sinners—the outcasts of the people of Israel. This practice earned him the title of a "drunkard and a glutton" from his enemies, which was, in some ways, to see him as the elder

19. See Crossan, *The Historical Jesus*, 69ff.

brother saw the prodigal son,[20] and it led to his rejection by the Jewish religious authorities, putting into motion the events that led to his crucifixion.

It is clear from the Gospel accounts that this was not an accidental practice of Jesus, but his intentional pursuit of outreach to the outcast of God's people—his attempt to draw them back within the healing embrace of God's tender care. When queried by the Pharisees about his practice of table fellowship with sinners, he responds, "Those who are well have no need of a physician, but those who are sick; I have come to call not the righteous but sinners to repentance" (Luke 5:31–32). This ministry, in other words, was his embrace of the prodigal son, his liturgy of reconciliation.

Luke's stories of Jesus' table fellowship with sinners are various—the feast with Levi (5:27–38), John and Jesus, the bridegroom and the ascetic (7:18–35); the anointing of Jesus' feet (7:36–50); the Pharisees' complaints (15:1–2); and the meal with Zaccheus (19:1–10)—but they share three common elements of gift, call, and repentance. Discerning the variable relations among these three elements within these stories helps us to understand the dynamics of Jesus' liturgy of reconciliation. Indeed, within the stories, we will find these three elements ordered differently, but upon closer examination, we will find that the element of gift—Jesus' gift of himself in fellowship—underlies each story and the Gospel narrative as a whole.

We can begin to uncover the relationship of gift, call, and repentance if we look at two stories that bracket Christ's meal ministry—the call of Levi at the beginning and the call of Zaccheus at the end. These two stories reveal the dynamics of gift, call, and repentance in their interactions with one another. Both stories are fairly simple. In the first, Christ has set out on his ministry, calling the people to repentance and belief in the kingdom, and he sees Levi, the tax collector (who, as a tax collector, would be a notorious sinner). He calls Levi to follow him, and Levi leaves everything. We immediately find Jesus at a feast at Levi's house, surrounded by tax collectors and other sinners. Here the Pharisees ask him how he can dine with sinners, and he responds with the above quotation about his mission to sinners.

In the story of Zaccheus, Jesus sees Zaccheus (a chief tax collector, or a king among sinners) in a tree and orders him down to play the host to Jesus. Again, there is grumbling about Jesus' fellowship with sinners. Zaccheus responds to Jesus' presence at his table by repenting of crimes against his people and promising restitution. Jesus declares that Zaccheus, a son of

20. See Feeley-Harnik, *The Lord's Table,* 77.

Abraham, has found salvation and reminds everyone of his own mission, still, to the sinful.

The dynamics of both stories are fairly straightforward. In the story of Levi, Jesus issues a call—to come follow him. Given the context of the story—Jesus' proclamation of repentance and the kingdom—we can assume that this proclamation was implicit in the call, so that Levi was responding to both. By leaving everything to follow Jesus, he is repenting of life in opposition to God's people (which was the reality of being a tax collector) and not only believing in Jesus' good news but joining himself to it. We can imagine that he did not yet understand what it was to which he had joined himself. Finally, Christ bestows himself as a gift to Levi and to the sinners who surrounded them, sitting at table with them in fellowship at a feast. It is a story of call, repentance, and gift.

In the story of Zaccheus, we find these elements ordered differently. Jesus calls Zaccheus to come down so that he can offer him his gift of fellowship. Zaccheus responds to this call and gift by first preparing a place for Jesus at table and then by repenting, seemingly in response to those who question Jesus' gift of himself to the sinful. Here the order is call, gift, repentance.

Both stories, then, begin with a call, but in one case, it is a call to repentance and commitment to the kingdom, while in the other it is the call to receive the gift of Christ's presence. Both stories, likewise, involve repentance, but in each the repentance is differently positioned, in one case preceding and in the other following the gift. Christ's gift of himself is positioned differently in the story, as well, but this gift, nonetheless, stands at the center of each story. This is evident within the stories insofar as the gift is the center of the controversy generated by the call, the gift, and the repentance. In both stories, it is Jesus' willingness to sit at table with sinners that evokes the anger of the Pharisees.

The centrality of the gift in these stories is more evident if we turn to a third story of fellowship that is only about gift. When Jesus is invited to dine with Simon the Pharisee, a notoriously sinful woman comes to wash his feet with her tears and anoint them with oil. Christ's willingness to allow this to happen—his gift of himself in receiving her love—arouses the ire of table companions, as we would guess.

In this story, Jesus' willingness to receive the woman's love is the whole of the action. There is no call, and though we might imagine that repentance was attached to the forgiveness by God that provoked her love, neither of these is anywhere noted. Again, the story is simply about Christ's gift of himself and the admittance of this woman, who is marked by her great love, into God's kingdom.

Embodying the Kingdom

What do I mean in terming Jesus' table fellowship in these stories as his gift of himself? We can clarify this if we return to the story of Levi for a deeper look at this gift. As we have observed already, Jesus' simple bestowal of fellowship in the story is a gift, since he declares his solidarity with his tablemates through this fellowship. And given that Jesus is a respected religious teacher (and Jesus was respected, at least by the people) and that he bestows his fellowship on the religiously outcast, he is bestowing the further gift of fellowship among the people of God.

In the story immediately following the story of Levi, the Pharisees wonder why there is such feasting among Jesus and his disciples, and Jesus replies that when the bridegroom is present, only a feast is appropriate. Jesus' presence at the table with the outcasts, then, bestows upon them not only fellowship with the people of God but a place at the table in the feast of the bridegroom—a place at the kingdom feast, if you will. In this way, finally, Jesus' table fellowship embodies the good news to which he called Levi and to which Levi responded. Jesus, in other words, does not simply proclaim that the kingdom of God is at hand, but through his presence as the bridegroom at table with those who have embraced this kingdom gospel, he turns their meal into a kingdom feast.

This final theme of embodiment is central to understanding Jesus' ministry and proclamation of the kingdom. In the story immediately preceding the feast with Levi, a paralytic is brought to Jesus, and Jesus pronounces his sins forgiven. When his authority to forgive sins is questioned, he manifests that authority through its embodiment in the healing of the man's paralysis. Jesus here doesn't simply preach the kingdom where the broken are healed; he realizes it, both spiritually and bodily.

So too in his table fellowship. Here he doesn't merely teach about the feast of the kingdom, but he also embodies it through his presence. Here the gift is not the healing of another's body but the gift of Jesus' own body at table. And as we shall see, he truly is offering his body here, since this gift of himself leads him to the cross and his death for these outcasts whom he has reconciled with God. When Jesus, therefore, explains in this story that he comes as a physician to heal the sinful, we must see that his fellowship, his presence, and his body are the medicine that he offers to enable this reconciliation. This is why I term it a liturgy of reconciliation.

Reconciliation and Repentance

Placing this emphasis on Christ's gift of himself in his ministry to the outcast—to the younger son of the parable—does not devalue repentance in these stories. It only recognizes that repentance here is dependent upon the gift; it is located in an orbit around the gift.

Jesus' teaching on his ministry of reconciliation in Luke 15 makes this more evident. This is the chapter where we find the Parable of the Two Sons, but this parable is preceded by two others—the stories of the man who seeks his lost sheep and the woman who seeks her lost coin. In both stories, it is the seeking after the lost and the joy in response to their recovery that is emphasized. The repentance of the sheep or the coin has no place in either story; indeed, it makes no sense even to wonder at its place. These two parables, then, form the context for our understanding of the Parable of the Two Sons and shape our understanding of seeking and repentance within it.

Interpreters often describe the central action of the Parable of the Two Sons as the repentance of the younger son and the gracious reception of that repentance by the father, who embraces the son once the son has realized his folly. This interpretation of the parable makes little sense on at least two levels. First, it belies the context of the parable in its relation to the parables of the Lost Sheep and the Lost Coin. If we are to understand these parables in parallel, then this reading of the prodigal would suggest that the first two parables should emphasize the effort of the sheep and the coin to return themselves to their owners, while the owner's joy would center on his or her good fortune at owning such a well-oriented sheep or coin. But that is not where the weight of any of these parables lies. Just as with the parables of the Lost Sheep and Coin the emphasis lay on the diligent care of the shepherd and housewife seeking out their beloved, so in the Parable of the Two Sons, the central dynamic is the searching, embracing love of the father who brings the lost son back into the family. It is the father's gift of his embrace that drives the story.

Moreover, we haven't understood the Parable of the Two Sons until we grasp the ambiguity of the son's so-called repentance that leads him to return home. Luke gives us several signals that we should look at this repentance with a cynical eye, all of them related to calculation behind the son's actions. We first need to note that the son's repentance is formulated in what we might call "self-talk"—the son "came to himself and said . . ." (Luke 15:17). Within Luke's Gospel, there are four other similar formulations of self-talk—the rich man, who counsels himself to build great barns to hold his harvest (Luke 12:13–21); the unjust steward, who counsels himself to defraud his master of contractual value to make friends for himself (Luke 16:1–13); the unjust judge, who decides to settle the widow's claim to buy himself some peace (Luke 18:1–8); and the arrogant Pharisee, who confides to himself in prayer that he is better than the nearby publican (Luke 18:9–14). Self-talk, in other words, is not the mark of sincerity or integrity in Luke's Gospel.

Admittedly, in the Parable of the Prodigal, we could read that he "came to himself and said ..." simply as "he came to his senses" and dismiss these other parallels. Further examination, however, suggests that we should not dismiss this connection so simply, for the younger son's conversation with himself resembles far more the conversations of the rich man, the unjust steward, the unjust judge, and the self-righteous pharisee—it is calculating, aimed at material gain, and shows little or no sorrow for the harm that he has caused others—than it does the uncalculated self-abasement of the publican. The father in the parable dismisses this so-called repentance, moreover, cutting off the son before he has even finished his well-rehearsed production.

Again, I am not arguing for a devaluation of repentance either in this parable or in Jesus' ministry as a whole. The parables of chapter 15 are told, after all, in response to pharisaical critique of Jesus' table fellowship with tax collectors and sinners who were coming to him—who were responding to his preaching—and this fits the emphasis on repentance that is a distinctive mark of Luke's Gospel.[21] Rather, I am simply pointing out the inherent incompleteness and ambiguity of all repentance.

Repentance is essential to the reconciliation that Jesus effects between God and God's people, but it is understood rightly only in its essential relationship to Jesus' gift of himself. There would be no reconciliation between the younger son and the father if the younger son did not return home, whatever his motives. But his life is truly changed only upon his return, if, when he is embraced by the father, he recognizes that home represents

21. See Johnson, *The Gospel of Luke*, 23.

not economic sustenance or benefit (his attitude on his first leaving and his return), but the enveloping love of the father.

Those tax collectors and sinners who gathered at table with Jesus could gather there only through some modicum of repentance. They required a desire to share table with the man of God. But their true repentance was possible only upon their reception of the gift of Jesus, which means that their repentance grew and deepened as they came to a deeper understanding and reception of this one who sat at table with them. This, indeed, is the heart of Jesus' call to repentance. The kingdom of God is near—the kingdom that was embodied in his table fellowship with sinners—repent in response to this kingdom that has embraced you and believe the good news that you experience.

Jesus and the Elder Son

Similar dynamics of call, gift, and repentance are evident in Jesus' meals with the religious authorities in Luke. Here, again, we find Jesus dining with sinners, but in this case the sin has an entirely different texture. It is the sin of the elder brother, who does not understand the love of the father or the nature of his fellowship, so that he rejects not only his younger brother but the father's love, as well. With this latter rejection, he, like the younger brother, has rejected the father. This is the case of the Pharisees and the scribes, as they are depicted by Luke. They have not only rejected the outcast of Israel—their brothers and sisters—but they reject the in-breaking of God's kingdom, of God's love, in God's embrace of the outcast through Jesus' table liturgy of reconciliation.

In response to their rejection of God's love for the outcast, Jesus responds in a way similar to the father in the parable—not by banishing them, but by reaching out to them in love, as well. Jesus offers himself to them in table fellowship—an offer of self that, again, will be fulfilled when they take him to Pilate to be crucified. Just as we must regard these religious authorities as sinners like those with whom Jesus dined throughout Luke, so we must understand Jesus' willingness to sit at table with them as a piece of his broader practice of table fellowship.

With this gift of himself at table came the consistent call to recognize the kingdom, to embrace the father's love for the younger son, to accept Jesus and his ministry to the outcast. It was a call to repent from their ways of exclusion, arrogance, and inattention to God's mission of love and to join themselves to the feast that God was hosting in and through Jesus.

Gift, call, and in response there was no repentance, at least as recorded by Luke. (We should note that John does record one Pharisee, Nicodemus, who is at least open to Jesus' call.) This lack of repentance does not break our pattern of the dynamic of Jesus' table fellowship, for one point of the stories of Jesus' meals with them is that they refused to repent. Repentance, in other words, is present in these stories by its absence.

What would a proper response to Jesus' call to the religious authorities have looked like? What would it mean to fulfill the call of the elder son? I suggested in the first chapter that this fulfillment was seen in Jesus himself. Here I will build on that suggestion and argue that in his instructions to his disciples to follow after his example, Jesus articulates explicitly the proper response of the elder son.

The father in the parable called on the son to come to share in his brother's return and reconciliation—his rebirth. An elder brother who was truly caught up in the spirit of the father's love would not have simply joined in this celebration but would have led in the preparations, even serving at the table. That, at least, is what we learn of the true elder son from the teaching of Jesus.

Across the Gospels, Jesus is found teaching the disciples that they are to pattern their lives after his. They are called not to lord their authority as his close followers over those entrusted to their care. Rather, they are to serve, even as he served. In each of the Synoptic Gospels, Jesus instructs his disciples on this matter in response to an argument among them over who is the greatest (Matt 20:25–28; Mark 10:42–45; Luke 22:24–30).

Luke's Gospel, however, is unique in placing this pericope after a meal—or, to be more specific, after Jesus' Last Supper with them. This editing of the story transforms Jesus' instruction to his disciples to be servants into a more specific call to serve at the table, as Jesus has served the outcast at table throughout his ministry. They, in other words, are not only to accept the in-breaking of God's kingdom through Jesus' table fellowship with the outcast, but are also to embrace and further that in-breaking by making Jesus' ministry their own.

By placing these instructions to serve after Jesus' Last Supper, Luke points us to a second conclusion beyond Jesus' call to serve at table. This placement also helps to solidify the connection of the Last Supper to the whole of Jesus' table ministry—the argument that we are presently exploring. It would be difficult to make the claim that Jesus, in this Last Supper meal, is calling on his disciples to set themselves apart from the unwashed in a manner like the Pharisees when they dine together, given his immediate instructions that they are to serve at the table—to join him in his table fellowship with the outcast. We see this point even more clearly if we turn to the one meal with the multitude where Luke wants us to see a specific parallel with the Last Supper, that is, the feeding of the 5,000.

In this meal, we see the disciples taking up the role that Jesus has commended to them, as they serve the gathered multitude with the bread that Jesus has blessed and broken. Given Luke's explicit signal of the eucharistic overtones of this meal—Jesus here takes, blesses, breaks, and gives the bread as he does at his Last Supper with his disciples—we cannot help but to read this as a command to the disciples to serve the outcast, the gathered, hungry multitude, at their eucharistic feast; and that they do this to remember Jesus, to make him present by embodying his ministry, the in-breaking of the kingdom, in their own lives and ministry.

If we turn to Mark's account of this meal with the 5,000 (Mark 6:30–44), moreover, we find it even more instructive for defining the place of Jesus' Last Supper in relation to his broader meal ministry. In Mark, the disciples have just returned from their mission preaching the gospel to the countryside, and we're told that Jesus calls them away to a quiet place, to reflect on their mission and, presumably, to share fellowship with one another. But a crowd follows them there, disturbing their quiet retreat. As the end of the day nears, the disciples remind Jesus of their desire to share a quiet meal together, and Jesus responds that their first call is to feed those who come to them hungry. And so the crowd is gathered on the grass, and the disciples serve at a Eucharist—at a kingdom feast where the multitude are fed—while Jesus presides.

A popular interpretation of Jesus' Last Supper argues that this meal among intimates stands apart from Jesus' broader practice of table fellowship—that it culminates a series of meals between Jesus and his disciples and that Jesus' command to do this is a command to continue this practice of intimate, exclusive meals. Yet this suggestion has little support in the biblical text. Not only are we offered no set of stories narrating Jesus' practice of sharing table fellowship with his disciples apart from the crowds, but we also find in the one place where the disciples suggest such an exclusive feast, Jesus rebukes them and asks them to be the true elder brothers, serving those who have come to them hungry and lost.

When Jesus asks his disciples to break bread and share table fellowship to remember him, he is clueing them into the essential role that his practice of table fellowship must play in their understanding of his story. Luke has clearly taken this clue. Through it, we see Jesus' story as the story of the gift of himself in table fellowship to those who are alienated from his father—both those who are prodigal and those who have isolated themselves in pious observance—and we have noted that this gift of himself truly cost him his life.

We have seen, moreover, that this gift is closely tied to his call to repentance, but that the relationship between gift and repentance is chronologically variable. Repentance could either precede or follow the gift of fellowship. Theologically, however, it is evident that repentance is wholly dependent on the gift, though it is also necessary to some degree for the reception of the gift. Sinners could not dine with Jesus if they were not willing to come to the table; Pharisees who came to the table nonetheless missed out on the gift through their refusal to receive it. But the gift was given—Jesus sat at table with the outcast and the religiously devout—whatever degree of repentance had been offered or not.

We have, finally, been led to consistently name the gift that Jesus gives when he gives himself to be the gift of the kingdom he preached—that by giving himself at table, the kingdom was breaking in through a duly constituted kingdom feast. We can now turn to Jesus' eschatological teaching about the kingdom through the image of feasting to learn more about his practice of table fellowship and the practice that he commended to his disciples when he told them to continue in this fellowship in remembrance of him.

The Kingdom Feast

In Luke's Gospel, Jesus connects his Last Supper with his disciples to the feast of God's kingdom not once, but twice. He shares this reference with Mark and Matthew, but his doubling of it underlines his conviction that we can understand Jesus' last meal and, with it, his life as a whole only in its relationship to the coming of God's kingdom, particularly as that kingdom is manifested in a feast. This emphasis on the kingdom feast in Luke's Gospel coheres with Luke's emphasis on Jesus' meal fellowship within the context of his preaching of the kingdom. Indeed, we understand the preaching and the fellowship fully only as we understand them together through this metaphor of feasting.

Jesus teaches throuhout Luke's Gospel about the coming kingdom, primarily through his parables. The kingdom of God is like a mustard seed, we find, which from inauspicious beginnings blossoms out to provide shelter and sustenance for a multitude (Luke 13:18–19). It is like new wine that shatters its old containers and that may not be appealing to those who are used to an earlier vintage (Luke 5:37–39). The ethics of the kingdom are the surprising ethics of the unjust steward who is commended for using the goods of this world to make friends for himself and his master in the world to come (Luke 16:1–13).

Through the metaphor of the feast, however, Jesus focuses us on one aspect of God's in-breaking into the old ways of our history, one aspect of the inauspicious seed from which the great feast will emerge. This metaphor of the feast is rooted deeply in the scriptural tradition of the Jewish people. It lies at the root of their history, as Moses, Aaron, and the seventy elders feast before God when God makes covenant with them at Sinai (Exod 24:9–12). It is also promised in their history's fulfillment, as God promises at the last day to make a feast for all people of rich food and well-aged wines on the mountain of the Lord (Isa 25:6). Implicit in the metaphor is the theme of great bounty and fellowship with God—a restoration to Eden, if you will, as God reconciles with God's people and showers them with God's blessing.

Jesus appropriates these themes into his kingdom parables of feasting, but his emphasis lies on the surprising guests present for this bounteous fellowship with God. "People will come from east and west, from north and south, and will eat in the kingdom of God," he teaches, though many in Israel will be locked outside of the banquet (Luke 13:29). He is concerned here with those who presume their place at the feast but who refuse to repent at his preaching of this surprising kingdom. The surprise of the kingdom, however, that the master will ask his servants to bring in the lame, the poor, the crippled, and the blind (Luke 14:16–24), functions consistently as the punch line of the parables.

One aspect of the surprise, in fact, is the outreach of the kingdom not only to the outcast of Israel but to the nations—again, people will come from east and west, north and south—an outreach presaged in Jesus' interactions with the Syro-Phoenician woman, who reminds him of the place even for dogs at the table (Matt 15:27). This inclusion of the nations makes Jesus' understanding of the kingdom consistent with Isaiah—that "on this mountain the Lord of hosts will make a feast for all people" (Isa 25:6). If in the Parable of the Two Sons we hear of God's intention to reconcile with the unwashed of God's people through God's invitation to the feast, we're instructed in these parables that "God's people" is an inclusive term that embraces all the nations.

Within Luke's Last Supper narrative, the timing of the kingdom feast to which Jesus looks forward is ambiguous. Jesus twice states his anticipation of a feast that celebrates the fulfillment or coming of the kingdom, but this anticipation could have two referents. Within the context of Luke's story, it could refer to that meal at the last day, when folk come from all directions to dine with Abraham, Isaac, and Jacob, or it could refer to that table fellowship that Jesus asks his disciples to continue in remembrance of him, given that he would have understood himself to be present to them at table through this remembrance.

This ambiguity is studied, not accidental, in Luke; it would, perhaps, be more appropriate to term it an intentionally multiple referent. By this placement of Jesus' perspective on the coming kingdom in his institution of this remembrance meal, we are asked to hold together the disciples' continued table fellowship in the presence of the remembered Jesus with the fulfillment of all of their feasting in the new heaven and earth of the kingdom. Their continued table fellowship becomes a manifestation of its final fulfillment; it is a foretaste of what is to come, and in that taste it offers a concrete promise of its bountiful fruition.

What holds these two instantiations of the feast together in the life of the church, of course, is the resurrection of Jesus that they both celebrate. In Christ's resurrection, Luke's community sees the victory of God's kingdom—its fulfillment. In their meals together in the presence of the remembered and resurrected Jesus, they have a foretaste of the new life in the kingdom that the resurrection promises. In their meals together, they manifest the new heaven and earth of the resurrection as they are the community of the resurrection.

Whether or not we believe that the Jesus of history could have named the event of his resurrection as the outcome of the suffering that was to follow his Last Supper, it is clear that he expected and taught his disciples to expect his vindication and the vindication of God's kingdom that he preached. And it is also clear that he taught that this vindication would represent the victory of new life, through which he would be present to his followers in the kingdom feast, both in their continued table fellowship and at the last day. The meal that Jesus asks his disciples to share in remembrance of him is, therefore, a meal celebrating the victory of the new life of the kingdom.

We need to recognize, however, that Jesus, through his teaching and ministry, taught his disciples to expect a certain shape to this new life—a shape defined by the surprising guests present at the kingdom feast with Jesus. In these guests, we see that *the new life of the kingdom is the new life of reconciliation*. It is the life of the prodigal who, once dead, is now alive—is now resurrected with Jesus—through the power of the father's love that has embraced him. The kingdom feast is the fruit of this reconciliation—those who come from west and east, north and south do so presumably because they have been reconciled with God. But it can also be seen as the catalyst of reconciliation. It is through the feast that the father seeks to reconcile both the prodigal and the elder brother to his love.

We recognize this reconciling shape of the kingdom feast, moreover, not only through Jesus' teaching on it but also in his embodiment of it by his ministry of table fellowship. Jesus' table fellowship is also caught up in the eschatological relationship between the meals of Jesus' followers in remembrance of him and the kingdom feast on the last day. The table fellowship commanded at the Last Supper, after all, is a continuation of the fellowship of Jesus with sinners that we have discussed above; and as we have seen, his pattern of fellowship in his ministry perfectly manifests the shape of the kingdom that he proclaims in his parables. In both cases, the kingdom is celebrated by those gathered off the street, while those who expected to be present for this feast have absented themselves from it through their own rejection or preoccupation. For this reason, Jesus' table fellowship has been described by many scholars as a prophetic act, presenting concretely the reconciling shape of the kingdom that he preaches.

Our analysis, however, suggests that we should speak more strongly of this table fellowship in its relationship to the coming of the kingdom. Just as Jesus was ambiguous at his Last Supper about the timing of the kingdom feast, so we find this same ambiguity of reference throughout his ministry. He can, on the one hand, speak of the kingdom as a future event to which he looks forward, as he does at the Last Supper. We find throughout Luke, on the other hand, the conviction that expectations for the coming kingdom were fulfilled in Jesus (see Luke 4:18–19; 7:22–23), while Jesus himself proclaims the kingdom to be already among the people (Luke 17:21). Jesus' table fellowship, in this light, should be seen not simply as a prophetic act, pointing us to a future kingdom, but as itself a realization of that kingdom in our midst. The feast of Jesus with sinners was the feast of the kingdom.

This recognition has implications for how we view the kingdom feast and its relationship to Jesus' Last Supper. We must see this feast for which we hope as simply and purely a feast for a motley crew, much as the Last Supper itself. It is a feast filled with the unwashed, the lost, the broken, and the unfaithful, and this in no way detracts from the feast. Indeed, from Jesus' perspective, it was a part of the kingdom's fulfillment. The kingdom of God that breaks in through Jesus is a kingdom that calls God's children to be reconciled to God through their participation in that kingdom, not in order that they may participate in the kingdom. *It is a kingdom of new life because it creates new life as much as it celebrates it.*

This recognition of the relationship between Jesus' preaching of the kingdom and his table fellowship will also have implications for how Jesus asks to be remembered. Jesus is the one who brings the kingdom, but who does so through his fellowship with those in need of reconciliation. The fullness of God's kingdom to which Jesus directs his disciples is the fullness of this reconciliation. By celebrating the kingdom meal, the disciples with Jesus present the world with the in-breaking of the kingdom and its life to which they are invited. The world is then left to respond to this life as they will.

The disciples in their continued table fellowship in remembrance of Jesus become the community of the resurrection not only through their celebration of his resurrection, but also through their enactment of it when they participate in the reconciling kingdom feast with those alienated from God. Resurrection here is not simply something that happens to Jesus after his ministry and death; it is also the fulfillment of the new life realized throughout Jesus' ministry in his offer of himself. This brings us to the third strand of meal traditions that informs Luke's account of Jesus' Last Supper—the paschal strand that has occupied so much Christian reflection for the past 2,000 years.

Jesus and the Paschal Feast

The paschal context is in many ways the most obvious for understanding Jesus' last meal with his disciples. All four Gospels, with Paul, emphasize this context in their interpretive presentation of this event. As I have argued, whether or not this meal was, in fact, a Passover seder, it makes sense that

Jesus would appropriate Passover themes in his preparation of his disciples for his coming death and the advent of God's kingdom, given the proximity of his death to the feast. Surely this connection did not occur only to the disciples and only after the fact. The question before us is what this paschal context adds to our understanding of Jesus' last meal and of his life and ministry through that meal, given all that we have seen up until now.

We need to begin by reminding ourselves that Passover was, first and foremost, a celebration of God's victory. It is a festival in the life of the Jewish people whose story culminated most immediately in the song of Moses—"I will sing to the Lord, for he has triumphed gloriously; horse and rider he has thrown into the sea" (Exod 15:1)—and which climaxed finally with the entrance into the promised land.

The hope of Passover is captured clearly in Luke's rendition of Jesus' last meal. We have seen this in our previous discussion, in Jesus' anticipation of the fulfillment of the kingdom that he both proclaimed and enacted in his ministry. Moreover, in Luke's account, when Christ's followers share table fellowship after their experience of his resurrection, we consistently find the celebration for God's victory in and through Jesus, especially as his presence and power were working through them. Through a paschal interpretation of this meal, followers of Jesus are asked to see God's glorious triumph as God has delivered God's people through Jesus' life, ministry, and death. Given what we have seen about Jesus' eschatological understanding of that deliverance, moreover, followers of Jesus must understand that they participate in its "already" while they await the "not yet" of its final fruition.

The paschal context of this meal adds another dimension to our understanding of Jesus' enactment of God's kingdom, however, through the themes of sacrifice and covenant that pervade it. Again, the story of God's deliverance of God's people begins with the sacrifice of the paschal lamb, through which God marks God's people and sets them apart for God's deliverance from the angel of death, and it celebrates an intermediate climax in the formation of God's people through the sacrifice and feast of the covenant ceremony at the foot of Sinai. The prominence of the paschal sacrifice was magnified through the practice of the Jewish people in Jesus' time, as thousands of lambs were slaughtered on the altar in Jerusalem as a prelude to this feast of deliverance.

These themes of sacrifice and covenant are notably invoked in the story of Jesus' last meal, and so they have dominated the church's understanding of this meal for two millennia. Jesus, Luke reports, offers his disciples bread as the gift of his body for them, and he offers them wine as his blood poured out for a new covenant. In this offering, Jesus' followers are taught to see his impending death as his gift of himself for their deliverance, and to understand his life, poured out in that death, as the seal on God's new covenant with God's people—the covenant through which they are ushered into the promised land of the kingdom that Jesus enacts.[22]

For Luke, this paschal understanding of Jesus' last meal in its relation to his death on the cross stands at the heart of the church's faith. Hence the echoing of the fourfold action on which he focuses our attention in his account of the feeding of the 5,000 in the midst of Jesus' ministry and his account with the two disciples at Emmaus, when the resurrected Christ is fully revealed and understood. But we fully grasp what Luke tells us through this meal about Jesus, his life, death, and resurrection only as we link this paschal focus to all else that we have understood about this meal.

We must first grasp that Jesus' gift of himself, as symbolized by his offer of bread, does not begin on the cross; the cross is, rather, the climax of this gift. The cross culminates and results from Jesus' offer of himself throughout his ministry in table fellowship with sinners. He offers himself to the outcast of God's people, invoking the wrath of the religious authorities, and he also offers himself in fellowship to those very authorities who will betray him at the hands of Pilate.

This self-gift of Jesus, as we have seen above, is central to his ministry—it is his liturgy of reconciliation at table with God's people. That Jesus symbolizes this self-gift through his offer of bread at a Passover seder (according to Luke) helps us to see the intersection of the paschal theme with Jesus' broader practice of table fellowship that defines his life. Jesus is the paschal lamb through whom we are delivered into God's embrace not only at his death, but through all of his days.

We must next recognize, as I argued in the previous section, that we can only understand the promised land into which Jesus delivers us, the company with whom we are delivered, and the covenant that binds us together if we hold together the land, company, and covenant with all that Jesus taught and enacted through his ministry. Jesus is clear there that through the in-breaking of God's kingdom, God's covenant has been opened to all—to the outcast, the unclean, the prodigal, the Gentile.

---

22. Luke Timothy Johnson offers an excellent, concise exegesis of Jesus' last meal with his followers in Luke as it relates to these paschal themes. See Johnson, *The Gospel of Luke*, 340-43.

It has, moreover, been opened not so that it can immediately be closed around this new company of God's people. Jesus has not poured himself out to create a new group of insiders who celebrate God's mercy apart from the whole of God's children. Rather, it is a covenant that ever seeks God's children, that ever invites them to become participants in that covenant through their participation in the covenant feast. They are to taste and see that the Lord is good and thereby to join themselves to the fellowship of God's people.

Jesus, finally, defines the law through which the covenant people are governed immediately after the covenant feast of his Last Supper (much as we find in Exodus 24). There he instructs his followers that they have been called not to recline at the table of this feast, but to serve at it, as he has served. They are, in other words, to offer themselves to the world just as their master has offered himself.

Luke Timothy Johnson is right to note an intimacy and bond that Jesus displays toward his disciples at this last meal.[23] But we mistake the character of this bond and intimacy if we think that it marks them off as the special and distinct recipients of Jesus' gift of himself. Jesus has repeatedly offered this gift to any and all who would sit at table with him. Through their reception of the gift of Jesus, some were moved to join themselves to the company of his followers—to repent and believe in the gospel. Others were not.

Jesus' followers are bound to Jesus *through the possibility of their joining Jesus in his offer.* They must recognize that they offer Jesus for the life of the world, but they must know that they can offer Jesus only through their offer of themselves, as they are joined to him through the covenant of his blood. They also have to know that this offer may be accepted or refused.

Taken, Blessed, Broken, and Shared

On the night before he died, Jesus gathered at table with his disciples, and he took the bread, blessed and broke it, and gave it to his disciples, saying, "This is my body, given for you. Do this for the remembrance of me." What is this clue to our understanding of Jesus that he offers to his disciples through Luke's account? What do we discover about Jesus through this juxtaposition of his Last Supper with the whole of his story? Principally, we have found that the gift of Jesus—as the one who himself was taken,

23. Ibid., 341.

blessed, broken, and shared by God—lies at the heart of the gospel. This is how Jesus understood his own story. It is the story of his gift of himself for us, and this gift and the ends for which it was given pervade every element of the story.

It is a gift that was given not only on the cross but throughout the ministry that led him to the cross, especially as he gave himself at table with sinners. The purpose of this gift is what I have termed Jesus' liturgy of reconciliation. As he gave himself at table to any who would join him, he was offering them the embrace of God and asking them to live into that embrace. It was a gift, therefore, that led to a call. The gift, by its very nature as embrace, challenged its recipients to turn from their rejection of God's love and to join themselves to God's embrace, both in their return to God and in their turning to one another in self-giving love.

Through this gift, Jesus enacts God's kingdom. He makes already present there at table with him a fullness of the life of love yet to be fulfilled in its entirety. This kingdom is a kingdom of resurrection. It is the in-breaking of God's touch into a dead and broken world, manifesting life through this feast of reconciliation. It is, as such, inherently a motley kingdom. It exists in and for the outcast, the lost, the prodigal who have drifted far from God, and this is the fullness of the kingdom—that they are invited to be present for the feast through which they can be transformed by the embrace of God.

This is the hope inherent in the love of God—that the feast which serves as the fulfillment of God's reign stands not only as the end of God's love but also as a means for the ever continuing outreach of that love. God's love has no end but is always inviting God's children to more and challenging them to turn and embrace that more.

When Jesus invites his disciples to do this to remember him, he is inviting them to continue in a practice of table fellowship through which the kingdom is embodied and through which he is present in that embodiment. He is asking them to allow him to continue to give himself to those alienated from God as an embrace and a challenge to accept that embrace. And he is asking them to join themselves to that gift, to serve at table as he served, to give themselves as he gave himself. He is asking them to continue his liturgy of reconciliation through their continued practice of table fellowship together and with the outcast, the unwashed, the prodigal, and the lost.

This is what Jesus has taught us about himself through his command to do this, at least as it is presented in Luke's Gospel. He has offered us a path through his story that casts his story as his liturgy of reconciliation through his gift of himself at table with the prodigal. We now need to ask how this story should shape our story or, more specifically, how his story shapes our understanding of our practice of the Eucharist through which we remember and make Jesus present in our midst. How do we share in this liturgy of reconciliation, this embodiment of the kingdom?

CHAPTER 3

A Theology of the Open Table

Man is a hungry being. But he is hungry for God. Behind all the hunger in our life is God. All desire is finally desire for Him. . . . The whole creation depends on food. But the unique position of man in the universe is that he alone is to bless God for the food and the life he receives from Him. He alone is to respond to God's blessing with his blessing.

—ALEXANDER SCHMEMANN, *FOR THE LIFE OF THE WORLD*

"DO THIS FOR THE remembrance of me." For 2,000 years, Christians have been invited to sit at table with Jesus, they have received Jesus' gift of himself and God's embrace in that gift, and they have faced the choice of accepting or turning from that gift. Through embrace, invitation, and acceptance, they have been reconciled to God. They have sat at the table with Jesus and been welcomed into fellowship with God. They, moreover, have been given the opportunity to share God's embrace with a broken world, to join Jesus as servants at the table inviting the alienated and the outcast into this blessed communion.

This, at least, is what many Christians have found as they have remembered Jesus at table. Their practice of his meal has opened for them this understanding of his story, and so they have opened their tables. They have recognized that they cannot be true to the memory and presence of Jesus in this meal unless they embrace and invite to the feast the unwashed prodigal, even as they, though prodigal, have been embraced and feasted.

This is the dynamic of the theology outlined in the chapter 2—that as we encounter Jesus at table, we are led to ever new, ever deeper rememberings of him and his story; and these, in turn, shape our continued practice of fellowship with him.

In the previous chapter, I explored how Jesus' own table liturgy, and implicitly our participation in it, shapes our understanding of his story. In this chapter, I will turn to the question of how the understanding of Jesus that emerges from a juxtaposition of his practice with his story shapes our continued participation in his liturgy. I will explore an articulation of a eucharistic theology of the open table through a consistent reference to the Christology—the understanding of Jesus—developed in the previous chapter. Indeed, the rootedness of this practice in an understanding of Jesus is one of its hallmarks.

It is, moreover, a practice bound intimately to a second christological practice, that of baptism, through which the open table comes to its fruition in our lives. But in order to fully appreciate the connection between Eucharist and baptism, we must spend some time explicating the details of this practice in its complex relationship to Jesus' story. To understand this practice, we need a rich understanding of our remembrance of Jesus and his presence at our table. We must tease out the nature of the sacrifice that undergirds the practice and the covenant relationship that it marks. We must honor and attend to the crisis inherent within our practice, as we are brought into God's presence, while recognizing the nature and dynamic of the grace that both precipitates this crisis and negotiates our way through it. From all of this, we will see the significance of both our place at the table with Jesus and our intentional attachment of ourselves to Jesus in baptism. Through this attachment, we join Jesus in his service at the table.

Initially, though, we need to discern more fully the motive force (the force that moves us) that enlivens this process of reconciliation and fellowship. If at the table we remember Jesus, we find that this memory is effective in our lives because it resonates with an older, deeper memory—our memory of God. That is the longing evoked by Jesus' invitation to sit at table, the longing for fellowship with God. Indeed, Jesus' practice of table fellowship was offensive to the religious authorities because he recognized this longing in the tax collectors and sinners who surrounded him, and so he allowed them some fulfillment of this longing by inviting them to the table of God's blessing.

At this table, then, we do not come to know God for the first time; rather, we remember the God whom we have known from our creation. We remember the God with whom we once walked in the garden at evening but from whom we are now alienated. This is one intuition about our remembering of Jesus at table that has led many to open their table—that in it we discern a memory of and desire for God that lies, however inarticulate, distorted, or misguided, at the depths of our being. Memory stokes desire and desire preserves memory; and so to understand our practice of Jesus' table fellowship, we must first explore the intricate psychology of memory and desire that drives it.

Longing and Thanksgiving

We can term this nexus of memory and desire *longing*. Longing is a movement of mind, heart, and will that receives depth from memory and intensity from desire, and it funds so much of the pathos and richness of life. This theme of longing recurs in discussions of opening the table, both among its practitioners and its detractors. The focus of this discussion tends to fall on the longing of those whom we invite to the table—how we should understand it and best respond to it.

Congregations that open their tables, however, have perceived in the story of Jesus a dynamic of longing that is more multidimensional than this singularly focused discussion suggests. These congregations are aware that they open their table as much as a response to God's longing for us and to their own longing for others. Opening the table, in other words, is born of a mutuality of longing; and if we return to the Parable of the Two Sons, we will find that it can help us understand this mutuality in the intricacy of its analysis.

The Parable of the Two Sons is throughout a profound meditation on longing. In fact, we have missed the depth of the parable until we attend to this. To focus our attention most fully, I will grant myself some homiletical license in my explanation of it. Jesus establishes clear emotional landmarks in his parables, but he does little to explore the terrain that these landmarks establish. We hear in this Parable of the desolation of the younger son, of the compassion of the father, and of the anger of the elder son, but we are left to discern the coherence of feeling to which these emotions belong. They all bespeak a longing for communion, a desire for relationships of mutual embrace, of knowing and being known, of celebration and compassion through which we can find ourselves by finding the other. They outline for us the dimensions of our longing for the kingdom.

This longing is most evident in the younger son, at least by the end of his journey. His journey into the far country begins as an excursion into frivolity, but it is transformed by the forces of the world into a passage into truth. The problem of a dissolute life is that it leads to our dissolution; and when the younger son comes undone, the most that he can hope for is a return home for material sustenance and safety.

But underneath his sad realism is the glimmer of the something more that home promises—the possibility of family, the hope of reconciliation, the yearning for the embrace. The younger son cannot articulate these. They are distant from him because they are out of his effectual grasp. He cannot make for himself the family that he unmade with his earlier decisions, but their reality remains alive in his longing. The seed of his father's love, implanted at his birth, has not died as it lay buried in a fallow field.

The longing of the father is evident not only in the compassion with which he sees his lost son return, but also in the speed with which he pursues his embrace. It is a puzzle to me whether his life in the years between his son's exodus and return has been one of mourning or expectant hope. His son was dead, lost to the world, beyond the father's reach, it seems from the parable. Yet the immediacy of the father's response to the return of the son hints that he has been waiting with hope, searching the horizon for the resurrection that he reports when it occurs.

I'm left with the impression that the power of his love enabled the father to see through the haunting reality of death in which the family was trapped to the life that lay beyond it. It was his love, after all, that worked this resurrection; the son was alive to the family again not because he returned, but because his aggrieved father embraced him. This was the power of his longing. The father shows us longing as a love that can acknowledge reality in all of its pain—he is clear that his son had died—while effecting its transformation.

The longing of the older brother is the most obscure. We are overtaken in the parable by his self-centered pity and his bitterness at the emptiness within which he has lived, dutifully tending to the business of the family while bereft of the joy that comes with the feast. The older brother, as I said before, misunderstands so much.

The feast that he has longed for has been his all the time. He has shared all with the father. He has shared life and love. This is the feast. The power to make this feast, for which he longs, this has been his as well. In sharing all with the father, he also could share the father's love and its power to work resurrection through reconciliation. He could share the seeking and the embrace.

And in longing for the power to make the feast, he misses the power of longing for his younger brother. He misses that there is no feast without him—that he, the elder brother, will be incomplete until the younger brother is restored. The elder brother misunderstands so much, including the true nature of his own longing, and so the father must be longing for the transformation of the elder son along with the return of the younger.

The Eucharist is a practice rooted in longing. Alexander Schmemann argues that human persons are, by nature, hungry creatures.[1] We are hungry for God, and we have been given this world to sate that hunger—not that by devouring the world we are satisfied and no longer desirous of God, but that in receiving the world we can turn to give thanks to God. For Schmemann, we were created for Eucharist, for a thanksgiving that feeds—both satisfies and stokes—the desire for God within us. This giving thanks to God over our meals—remember the importance of the *berakah* at the beginning of the meal in Jesus' Jewish context—is our communion with God.

Our fallen state, then, is defined by our love and consumption of the world for itself, neglecting to give thanks for it to God. We seek communion only with the world and not with God, so that the world becomes opaque to the God whose presence it was to mediate. We have consigned ourselves to "a non-eucharistic life in a non-eucharistic world," Schmemann will say, and through this dissolution our desire is starved, both heightening the pang of our hunger and numbing us to it.[2]

Those who come to Jesus' table come with this hunger. This is one interpretation of what we saw in Jesus' story, that both sinner and Pharisee had lost their capacity for eucharistic living and operated out of a hunger instilled by this loss. We, too, baptized or not, church member or not, have dissipated our attentiveness to God's presence and wander in a wilderness of God's absence.[3]

But when we come to the table hungry, we are received there like the prodigal, not like Esau—we don't abandon our birthright in order to be fed but receive it through the meal. In the parable, the prodigal was not

---

1. See Schmemann, *For the Life of the World*, 14–18.

2. Ibid., 18.

3. See Lathrop's discussion of the Eucharist in *Holy Things*, especially 119ff.

only fed, but he was also restored to his family through the feast, so that he might for the first time recognize the desire for family that had been at the heart of his poverty. This is the truth of our longing as we are lost in the world. Our memory of God fades and our desire for God is dampened in our forgetfulness. It is the embrace of the Father that revives them both.

Presence at the table, then, begins to satisfy our hunger, but only after it has first awakened it. This is the dialectic of longing that runs not only through our celebration of the Eucharist but also through the whole of the Christian life. Eucharist, prayer, service to the poor, fellowship—these all feed our hunger for God as they allow us to give thanks to God for the grace God has bestowed upon us.

They feed this hunger, however, not to extinguish it, but to allow us through this satisfaction to realize the depths of the hunger within us.[4] The Christian life nurtures hunger even as it nourishes it. In the parable, the younger son is welcomed to the table, and his hunger for family is awakened and fed; but surely we cannot read this parable without recognizing the depth of further reconciliation and growth that must take place for the son to realize his full place in his father's house. We see, moreover, that once this initial reconciliation has been effected, there is the further growth of hunger and its nourishment to be realized so that the younger son might come into the place of the true elder son—the son who has made the father's love his own.

We are invited to the table, and we invite others to the table so that we might feed and deepen our longing for God. We are mistaken if we believe that this longing is fully satisfied by a simple meal, but we are also mistaken to think that this longing, hidden so deeply within our breasts, can even come to surface unless it is first fed and given hope for satisfaction at the welcome table of the Lord. Again, Christian life both nurtures and nourishes the hunger for God within us, and this nurture and nourishment begin at God's table. Hence the call to open our tables.

Reading this practice within the context of the Parable of the prodigal, moreover, we must recognize that our hunger is awakened at the table

---

4. Farwell provides a rich discussion of longing and desire in the Christian life. See Farwell, "Baptism, Eucharist, and the Hospitality of Jesus," 233–35. There he describes how our participation in God both "satisfies and excites" our longing. "We are fed at the table, yet with a morsel of bread and a sip of wine that blesses our hunger as much as it satisfies it" (234). My disagreement with Farwell is rooted in my perception that the practice of the open table depends on this dynamic of longing; it is not an attempt to subvert it.

because it is met there by the hunger of the father, the hunger of God for us. Practitioners of the open table do so because of the longing they find in those who come to their churches. More principally, though, they do so on account of the longing that they find within their community, and by this I mean not their own longing, but the longing of God.

They hear God's proclamation of love for God's children:

> When Israel was a child, I loved him,
> and out of Egypt I called my son....
> It was I who taught Ephraim to walk,
> I took them up in my arms;
> But they did not know that I healed them.
> I led them with cords of human kindness,
> With bands of love.
> I was to them like those
> Who lift infants to their cheeks.
> I bent down to them and fed them. (Hos 11:1–4.)

They believe that God's yearning is not just for those who stand already within the fold of the church but for humanity as a whole. God longs for human persons, created for communion with God. Again, this is what we found in Jesus' story. He is the Son who has come to offer himself to the lost at table at the behest of the seeking love of the Father. He is the Father's embrace, the Father running out in joy to draw the lost into the feast. He is the hunger of the Father, incarnate, and we meet him, this hungering love, at the table.

This description of God's longing expressed in Jesus does not refer us to a passion that is weak and ineffectual. God's hunger or longing is not the longing of a high school teenager whose quest for true love is destined to go unfulfilled. It is, rather, the ever seeking, effectual working of God's love in the world. As Augustine wrote, "You called me; you cried out to me; you broke the barrier of my deafness. You shone upon me, your radiance enveloped me; you put my blindness to flight."[5] God's longing is the longing of the father whose love resurrected his son. God's heart is restless until we rest in God—this is the dynamism of the divine life in its mission to God's children—but the love that flows from this heart is an effective love that

---

5. Augustine, *The Confessions*, 254–55.

resides at the center of our table celebration. It is to this love that we beckon all comers.

The Eucharist, for practitioners of the open table, is the feast of God's longing. In their invitation to the Eucharist at St. Mark's in Washington, DC, they proclaim, "This is God's feast, and not our own. . . ." They see themselves as simply attending to the desire of God's longing.

This is doubly true if we return to our analysis of the parable, for there we saw that the father's longing was equally directed to the elder son—that he would rejoice and come to join the father in setting a feast for the return of the lost brother. God's longing is that we should long for one another—that we should long to join ourselves to the father's love in laying out the feast. This is the third dimension of longing in this practice, and it ties into the same dialectic of longing that I discussed above. Even as our longing for God is fed and nurtured at the table, so is our longing for one another.

At times in open table congregations, the invitation to the table directed to all can seem superfluous because no seekers, no visitors, none from outside of the community are present for the feast. But this invitation is experienced, nonetheless, as vital to their celebration. It expresses their own longing to be joined to God's longing. It expresses their own desire to include brothers and sisters whom they do not know in this thanksgiving meal. It expresses their own yearning that, in this world broken by so many divisions—political, social, racial, religious—they might be a community of reconciliation. This yearning is joined to the belief that reconciliation begins with an invitation to all to join them in their fellowship with Jesus.

The invitation to all to come and join the feast is for open table congregations a question of identity as well as a question of mission. Through their identification of themselves both with God's longing and with their brothers and sisters who live outside of their community, they identify themselves with Jesus, who is the incarnation of God's longing through his solidarity with those on the outside.

Perhaps, though, it would be more apt to make this point in reverse, that through our identification with Jesus at table, we are identified with God's longing and with the brothers and sisters who live outside of our communities. Again, we grasp this approach to the Eucharist only as we understand its christocentric texture. Thus, this theoretical discussion of longing becomes concrete when we turn to a discussion of our remembering of Jesus, through which we receive an awakened and sanctified memory of God.

Anamnesis, Presence, and Eucharist

At the heart of the church's prayer of thanksgiving, the congregation proclaims their memory of Jesus' death and resurrection and their hope for the fulfillment of his advent in their lives. "We remember his death, we proclaim his resurrection, and we await his coming in glory," Episcopalians cry out in their eucharistic Prayer B. In this proclamation, the church declares its faith in Jesus' gift of himself, in the life that God has established through this gift, and in the possibility of our participation in this life in its abundance. Increasingly this proclamation is placed in the context of a broader prayer that locates the cross as its focal point, while recognizing that Jesus' self-gift began with his incarnation and continues in his offer of himself to the world today.[6] The conception of Jesus' gift of himself is consistent with the fullness of his gift that we encountered in our analysis of his gospel.

When we remember Jesus, we are remembering principally his gift. We must note, however, the essential role of Eucharist, of giving thanks to God for this gift in our practice of memory. Indeed, this was the fundamental transformation of Jesus' table practice that determines our present rite. According to Luke, at Jesus' Last Supper with his disciples, he gives thanks to God—offers the *berakah* or makes Eucharist—over the bread and asks them to do this in the future in remembrance of him.

He assumes that they will continue to give thanks to God for God's gift of bread and the created order that supports them. He now includes within this *berakah* a remembrance of him—a thanksgiving for his gift of himself and the embrace of God that they have received through this gift. Dom Gregory Dix has argued convincingly that early Christian Eucharists are structured around the Jewish *berakah*, that they were essentially prayers of praise and thanksgiving to God for the gift of creation and of Jesus, through whom they were reconciled to God.[7]

Captured within our table practice, then, is this sense that Jesus has given himself to us at table, much as God has given us the world. He has given himself so that through this gift we might be blessed, recognize God in this blessing, and give thanks to God in return. Jesus' gift of himself, in

---

6. This broader understanding is consonant with the earliest eucharistic prayers that we find in the church's life—see Dix, *The Shape of the Liturgy*, 156–207.

7. Ibid., 208–25; see also Paul Marshall's "additional notes" in Dix, *The Shape of the Liturgy*, 769–71. Dix argues that the words of institution and the epiclesis—aspects of the prayer that later generations come to see as essential—were in fact later additions to this central core.

other words, is a revelation to us both of God's goodness and of our essential nature as eucharistic beings. Again, as Schmemann maintains, we are people hungry for God, and this hunger is fed as we give thanks to God at table for God's gifts to us, especially God's gift of God's embrace in Jesus.

This was what discriminated the response of the Pharisees, who remained alienated from God in their table fellowship with Jesus, from that of the sinners, who were reconciled to God through that fellowship. We saw in our exploration of Jesus' story that repentance in response to Jesus was an essential aspect of the reconciliation that Jesus effected, but underlying this repentance was the Eucharist with which Jesus' fellowship was received at table. Tax collectors received this fellowship with thanksgiving, offering themselves up to God in return for this blessing. For the scribes and Pharisees in Luke's Gospel, however, table fellowship with Jesus was a time for strife and self-serving arguments; there was no space for thanksgiving or a recognition of God's embrace in Jesus. Their fellowship was utterly noneucharistic.

This analysis fits as well the Parable of the Two Sons as I have understood it. I have noted that the lost son's return was marked by a repentance that was less than authentic, and that the father's embrace served as the true turning point in the life of the son. That this turning would take place, however, would depend on the son's reception of the embrace eucharistically and not with the greed that marked his reception of his father's bounty at the beginning of the story. Likewise, the elder son is alienated from the father even as he shares in this bounty because of his noneucharistic participation in the father's goodness. His life in his father's household is marked by duty and burden, not by joy and thanksgiving. He must as well recover his eucharistic center if he is to find life with his father.

At the center of Christian life, then, is the reception of Jesus' gift of himself and a eucharistic response to God for this gift, in return. When we remember Jesus, we are remembering his gift in order to make thanksgiving. Our thanksgiving will be full to the degree that our memory of the gift is full. For all that I have said about thanksgiving and memory of God, the action of the Eucharist begins where Jesus directed us, in remembering him.

We need to remind ourselves of all that is contained in this action. We consistently run the danger of constricting our memories as we recall Jesus. We can fail to recall the fullness of his life, we can fail to recall the fullness of his love, and we can, perhaps most importantly, fail to be mindful that this act of *anamnesis* is not a simple recalling. It is an opening of ourselves to the presence of the one whom we remember through that act of memory.

Our previous chapter was a beginning to the exercise of this fullness of memory. It reminds us that in remembering Jesus, we are not simply to remember his death and resurrection, though these certainly occupy a central place in our memory. We remember Jesus fully by remembering the shape of his life among us, a shape that provides the context for understanding his passion and victory in Jerusalem even as they provide the fulfillment of the story of his life.

It means, in the first place, that we are to remember Jesus at table. We are to remember Jesus at the place where life is nourished and the circle of God's blessing is constituted by our thanksgiving to God for God's gifts. We are to remember Jesus at table, moreover, with those alienated from God. He sits at table with the outcast—those who are unclean and so deemed unworthy for fellowship with God. He sits at table as well with those whose religious rectitude has transformed lives of thanksgiving into lives of arrogant, burdened duty that cuts them off from the newness of God's constant creativity. We are to remember in all of this Jesus' liturgy of reconciliation, that at table he offers himself as the embrace and call of God to the alienated, that they might embrace the life of God in him in return. This is the strange covenant, the radical kingdom that Jesus enacted in his life and table fellowship and that he sealed in his death and resurrection.

For the church in its very early days, remembrance of Jesus meant exactly this remembrance of the fullness of his life, for which they gave thanks. It was a memory that culminated with his cross and resurrection, where the fullness of his life is revealed—that he has given himself for our sakes and that through that gift he has won life for the world—but cross and resurrection embodied this centrality only in relation to the whole of his story.

Soon, however, the church's eucharistic memory of Jesus was constricted to the memory of his cross and resurrection as the church sought to ground its liturgical practice more deeply in the events of Jesus' passion, which gave this practice its authority.[8] The vibrancy of their symbolic power threw the broader sweep of his life into the shadows, diminishing the scope of our christological vision. The centrality of Jesus' gift and victory to our thanksgiving were not lost with this shift, but the true dimensions of both gift and victory, of the kingdom that Jesus inaugurated and sealed, were

8. Ibid., 230–37, especially 234.

occluded. This was never the intention of the shift but was, rather, one of those unintended accidents of change with which the history of liturgical practice is littered.

Contemporary awareness of the need to recover a more complete liturgical remembrance of Jesus is evident across the spectrum of the Christian eucharistic tradition. Witness to Jesus' death, resurrection, and coming advent is rooted ever more deeply in narration of his life and ministry and the coloring that they provide these culminating events. The church's liturgy has always drawn eucharistic attention to the reconciliation that Jesus accomplished for us, but it is all too easy for the surprise, the grace of this reconciliation, to be lost.

Witness to the fullness of Jesus' ministry, especially his ministry at table, reminds us that the elder brother stands with the younger brother in the presence of God—both are alienated from the love of God and both are recipients of the love of God, the embrace of the Father, in their fellowship with Jesus. As Gordon Lathrop reminds us, we find in the Gospels that Jesus always stands with the stranger to grace, the outsider, and that should be a discomfiting comfort to us, as we are reminded in this that we come to the table always as outsiders, but that it is precisely there, on the outside, that we are met by Jesus.[9] A full remembrance of Jesus reminds us that we all sit at table with Jesus only because his table is open, and so our thanksgiving at the table is grounded precisely in this openness.

The fullness of our memory of Jesus entails a second dimension as well. We are to remember not only the breadth and depth of his gift here at table but also the immediacy of that gift. To put it in Luke's terms, we, like the disciples at Emmaus, are not simply to recall Jesus but to know him in the breaking of the bread. Fundamental to the Christian understanding of eucharistic memory is the reality of Jesus' presence to the table fellowship in the breaking and sharing of the bread. So we are reminded repeatedly that this Greek word for remembering, *anamnesis*, means not a simple recalling but a making present. To say that we remember Jesus in this sense is to say that he is present to us in this memory.

We must take care in how we discuss this presence, however. We don't want to say that we make Jesus present in our remembering, for that seems to imply a dead Jesus whom we revive through our eucharistic action. Rather, we should say that we are made present to Jesus, that we are revived to his presence through the power of Jesus' gift to evoke our thanksgiving.

9. Lathrop, *Holy Things*, 119–22.

We are the ones who are changed in the Eucharist, not Jesus.[10] The Jesus whom we remember at table is the living Jesus, the Jesus of the resurrection, so that in our recollection of that resurrection, we are awakened to his reality in our midst.

The presence of Jesus through our memory is vital to the eucharistic understanding of the meal that we share. If our memory of Jesus is, in the first place, of his gift of himself at table and of the embrace of the Father that we receive through that gift, then the recognition of the presence of Jesus at table opens us to receive his gift, his embrace, in our sharing of the bread and wine. In remembering Jesus at table, we receive the embrace of God. In our continued participation in Jesus' table fellowship, we are continually reconciled to God. We are met by the longing of the Father in our memory of the gift of the Son, since in the memory we truly find the gift.

The presence of Jesus in our memory of him at table, then, reminds us that this is his table, not simply then, but now. It is his table of reconciliation, where he gathers with the alienated and outsider. Our choice is either to give thanks for that reconciliation, that we are gathered there with others, or to stand outside the gathering and not participate in the fellowship of grace.

Our memory of Jesus at table thus has an incarnational shape. It exists at the intersection of our recollection of Jesus' gift of himself in his ministry and death with our recognition of his living presence through the power of his resurrection. It is vital that we hold these two aspects of our memory of Jesus together in our celebration of his table fellowship. We must hold firm to the fact that the glorified Jesus with whom we dine in the Eucharist is the Jesus of the Gospels who stands with the outcast—the Jesus of the kingdom of the outsiders. At the same time, we must affirm that Jesus in his life and ministry was working resurrection—the dead were made to live through his offer of the embrace of the Father in his gift of himself.

It is tempting to sever Jesus' table fellowship in the Gospels from our fellowship with him now, to place the chasm of the resurrection between the promise of the former and the fulfillment of the latter. To do so, however, is to sever Jesus—to sever his glory from his humility, his gift from his victory. It is to divide our memory and with it our thanksgiving to God for God's willingness in Jesus to stand with us, the alienated, today as much as yesterday.

---

10. Hooker, *Of the Lawes of Ecclesiasticall Politie*, Book V.67, 338–40.

Sacrifice and Covenant

Schmemann argues that we understand the Eucharist aright only when we understand it as a way of life. It is not merely a cultic act. It does not stand apart from our daily lives in a sacred space where we appease the gods; rather, it centers our daily lives as it orients us to our relationship with God.[11] The Eucharist is a way of being in the world grounded on gift and thanksgiving. In the Eucharist, we celebrate the gift of God's love in the gift of this world and, more principally, in the gift of Jesus through our reception of those gifts with thanksgiving. This is a model of what it is to live eucharistically.

This way of life, moreover, flows out from our table fellowship. It is at the table that we receive Jesus' gift of himself in fellowship, and it is at the table that we can offer our *berakah,* our thanksgiving to God for the life that we receive in this gift. We need to constantly recall this emphasis on table fellowship in our understanding of the Eucharist, for it will serve to remind us that this practice is grounded in our memory of Jesus, in his practice of table fellowship, and of the openness of his invitation to that table, through which he gave himself to the world.

This emphasis on table fellowship or, more specifically, Jesus' table fellowship, bears on our understanding of two concepts central to the church's eucharistic practice—those of sacrifice and covenant. These are concepts by which this gift and this way of life are developed in the church's talk about its practice of remembering Jesus. These are powerful concepts, redolent with the rich aromas of ancient religion and our earliest explorations of the holy darkness in which we come to meet God, but they are also dangerous concepts that can lead us down the wrong path in our understanding of this meal through which we are, in fact, embraced by God. As Gordon Lathrop argues, they are in many ways wrong words taken up and broken in our liturgical practice so that they might speak most profoundly to the new thing of God's grace in Jesus.[12]

A notion of sacrifice is central to the eucharistic discourse of the church. It is grounded in the biblical language of sacrifice through which Jesus' death was understood from the beginning, and it binds to this language a recollection of our own need to offer ourselves to God as a fulfillment of our right relation with our creator. Yet this language can lure us

---

11. Schmemann, *For the Life of the World,* 25–26.
12. Lathrop, *Holy Things,* 142–43.

into the appealing notion that we have done what is necessary, either here in our liturgy or earlier on the cross of Calvary, to appease God—that we offer Jesus to God to earn our forgiveness. This mistakes who it is that offered Jesus. It forgets that our offering at the eucharistic table is an offering of thanksgiving. And it leads us to think of the Eucharist as primarily a cultic act—something that we do apart from the fullness of our day-to-day lives in order to insure those lives.

Likewise, the idea of covenant can yield an understanding of the eucharistic community as a closed community. We can all too easily see ourselves as the community of those who have entered into the new covenant sealed by Jesus, made acceptable to God through the offer of the proper sacrifice, over against those left on the outside. It is an understanding of covenant that belies the memory of Jesus that we uncovered in our previous chapter. There the new covenant was defined by its eternal openness to the outsider. We must beware when talking of Eucharist and covenant that we not recreate under the rubric of the new covenant the very notion of a closed religious community that Jesus attacked throughout his ministry.

Again, the language of sacrifice and covenant is integral to our understanding of the eucharistic feast that we celebrate around Jesus' table every Sunday. The danger of this language should not persuade us to impoverish our vocabulary through its omission. We must recognize, however, that we understand our liturgical practice aright only as we allow these notions of covenant and sacrifice to be defined by Jesus' story. They must be held in the context of Jesus' particular practice of table fellowship and our remembrance of that practice in the presence of the risen Christ.

If we begin with the language of sacrifice, we must first note with Lathrop the metaphorical nature of this term in our usage.[13] Our meal at Jesus' table does not equate to the ritual practice of sacrifice at the altar of God within either pagan religions or the biblical cult of the Old Testament. Similarly, Jesus' death outside the camp in the region of the unclean stands in many ways as the antisacrifice; it is a death that in its impurity undoes traditional notions of sacrifice. The recognition that we use "sacrifice" as a metaphor opens us to see this language in a new way. It allows us to speak the fresh grace of the gospel.

First, it undermines our tendency to equate our understanding of Jesus' death as sacrifice with any sacrifice that we might offer to God. Given the biblical interpretation of Jesus' death on the cross as a sacrifice, it is a

13. Ibid., 142.

short leap to see this sacrifice as one that we could claim through his human solidarity with us. Through the offer of this one man, so the argument goes, we all have made proper sacrifice to God.

This misses the singular nature of Jesus' offer of himself, a singularity better captured by the language of John's Gospel, where Jesus is called the Lamb of God. Jesus is God's lamb, God's sacrifice, not ours. Again, to return to the language of the Parable of the Two Sons, Jesus is the embrace of the Father, or better, the offer of the True Elder Son to pursue his lost siblings into the far country where he might communicate this embrace.

Here the context of table fellowship to clarify the cross is vital, for at table we are clear that Jesus' offer of himself is an offer to us to enter into the circle of God's fellowship, an offer or sacrifice made to us on God's behalf, not to God on our behalf. It reminds us, as Dix points out, that Jesus' sacrifice begins with his incarnation and continues into eternity in God's continual offer of fellowship to a broken and lost humanity.[14]

Second, the recognition that we use "sacrifice" as a metaphor helps us to understand the content of this sacrifice aright. At the heart of the religious use of the language of sacrifice is the renewal or consummation of human relation with God. This renewal involves two dimensions, however. The sacrifice is, on the one hand, a sacrifice for forgiveness. In Matthew's account of Jesus' Last Supper with his disciples, Jesus explains that his blood was poured out for many "for the forgiveness of sins" (Matt 26:28). It is tempting, again, to hear this in terms of our blood offering to God to cover our sins, but John's Gospel takes us in another direction.

Having clarified for us that Jesus is God's lamb, John later expounds the forgiveness that we find in the cross through a story of Moses and the people of Israel in the desert (John 3:14–16). Jesus recalls for Nicodemus the story of Moses lifting up an image of a serpent on a pole when Israel had fallen into unfaithfulness, so that all who turn to the serpent as a sign of God's mercy might be forgiven their unfaithfulness and live. So too, Jesus explains, he will be lifted up on the cross as a sign of God's mercy so that we might turn to him and find God's forgiveness through which we can return to God's welcoming embrace. When seen in this light, Jesus' sacrifice marks as much as it achieves God's forgiveness. It recognizes that Jesus was sent by God out of God's welcoming forgiveness to midwife our rebirth into fellowship with God.

14. Dix, *The Shape of the Liturgy*, 242.

Jesus' offer, then, manifests God's forgiveness as God's gift to us, and thereby marks the end of our cultic offerings by which we think that we can appease God. Jesus' sacrifice stands not as the one true fulfillment of the our previous sacrifices to God at the altar, as if to say, now we have offered that which is good enough, pure enough, to turn away God's wrath. Rather, it reveals that our forgiveness comes not from anything that we offer, but rather through God's provision. As in the story of Abraham's sacrifice of Isaac, we have found that God has provided for us apart from our gift, with a result that any attempt to win God's favor through our gift has ended.

Christians, then, can use this notion of sacrifice in relation to the Eucharist to understand how God has opened a way for us into relationship with God in the midst of our brokenness and the guilt intrinsic to it. In Jesus, we see that God has made a sacrificial offer of God's love, and in this offer, we find God's forgiveness, which opens a way for us to enter into relationship with God. Through all of this we see how Jesus' blood was poured out for many for the forgiveness of sins. Within the church's eucharistic discourse, however, Jesus' sacrificial offer of his life, as symbolized in the pouring out of his blood, is tied to a second, deeper reality in connection to the relationship that God initiates with us through Jesus' life, death, and resurrection.

In Luke's Gospel, as we observed earlier, Jesus proclaims that his blood, poured out, is the blood of the new covenant. Jesus, through his offer of himself, has not only opened our way to relationship with God through the forgiveness that he made manifest. He has also created this new relationship, this new covenant, this new way of being with God defined by God's embrace and our response to this embrace with thanksgiving and repentance.

Again, this is the pattern that we found in Jesus' table ministry—that he offers himself as God's embrace to those alienated from God. Those who receive this embrace with thanksgiving are led through it to a change of life, a new way of living in fellowship with God. Here Jesus' offer or sacrifice of himself doesn't simply mark the gift that we receive through it. It also establishes the gift. Jesus' offer of himself is God's reinitiation of relationship with us, and this offer establishes the dynamics of the relationship, of the covenant, in its sheer gratuity.

The church's eucharistic way of life, therefore, proceeds from this sacrifice as thanksgiving for the grace of Jesus' offer of embrace. The Christian community, at the same time, is defined by the covenant that this offer establishes. It is an open community, the outworking of God's mysterious kingdom whose goal is to recover all those of God's children who have alienated themselves from God's parental love. We can best recover the sense of Jesus' covenantal sacrifice if we return to God's first covenant with Abraham, the covenant, Calvin argues, that is the basis for all other covenants that God makes with God's people.[15]

In the Genesis 15, when God makes covenant with Abraham, God commands Abraham to sacrifice a heifer, a goat, a ram, a turtle dove, and a pigeon and to cut them in half, laying out the halves in two rows. As Abraham then sleeps, he sees God offer Godself in covenant to Abraham, passing through the sacrificed animals in the form of a firepot without asking Abraham to reciprocate. The meaning of the ceremony is to bind oneself in covenant to another, proclaiming, in effect, "May I be divided as these animals if I break covenant with you." In the ceremony, then, God unilaterally bound Godself to Abraham and those who would come after him. God creates a covenant that is unshakable, because it depends only on God's faithfulness and not on ours.

The broader content of the covenant that God seals with this ceremony can seem exclusionary on first reading. God assures Abraham that he will have a great family in this passage, and within the covenant promise is a commitment to Abraham of the promised land—the land that currently belongs to the Kenites, Hittites, Canaanites, and Amorites, among others. God promises here that these nations will be expelled from the land so that it might be possessed by Abraham's children. Thus, Abraham's children seem to stand in special relationship with God, as those chosen as God's children among all the rest.

But the broader context of this passage begins with God's promise in Genesis 12 to make of Abraham a great nation, so that through him "all the families of the earth shall be blessed" (Gen 12:3). This story comes at the end of the opening account of creation, as we see God's human creatures embracing the role of the prodigal, turning from God and squandering their birthright as those created in God's image for relationship with God. These first eleven chapters in Genesis end with the scattering of God's people and the confusion of their languages—the fulfillment of their dissipated lives. God's call of Abraham, then, is God's initial step in God's plan

---

15. For a detailed exploration of Calvin's understanding of God's covenant, see Edmondson, *Calvin's Christology,* 49ff.

for the reconciliation of the lost. God creates a covenant community into which the families of the earth might be engrafted when the time is right.

With Jesus, we see this plan and this covenant that began with Abraham brought to fulfillment. In Jesus, God again offers Godself in covenant unilaterally, creating a covenant grounded in God's faithfulness and not ours. It is also quite plainly a fulfillment of Abraham's call to be a blessing to all of the nations. It is a covenant directed not simply to Abraham's Jewish descendants but to all of God's children—to all of the prodigal. Finally, it is a covenant that requires the repentance of thanksgiving as a response to God's unilateral offer. It requires nothing other than a willingness to accept God's offer of fellowship in Jesus with gratitude.

This is the promised land to which Jesus would lead us—the space of table fellowship with God, active membership in the family of God. We enter simply by taking a seat at the table and accepting the welcoming embrace of the Father. Having entered, we have embraced on our part a way of life defined by our thanksgiving to God for God's gift, not by our own achievements, our own Babel towers, religious or secular, through which we seek to storm heaven.

The new covenant founded on Jesus' sacrifice is, thus, not only unshakable but also fundamentally open. Indeed, its requirement, as we saw in the fellowship of Jesus with the Pharisees, is an acceptance of its openness, its foundation on God's grace through which all are welcome, rather than a reliance on our own religious achievement or rectitude through which we might define ourselves over against our siblings—those we label as the prodigal.

The practice of opening the Eucharist table is the practice of the new covenant. It is a practice grounded in the forgiveness of God revealed in Jesus' offer of himself, and it is the actualization of the covenant fellowship established by Jesus in this offer. It is a reception of God's gracious offer of reconciliation with thanksgiving, manifesting its recognition of that grace through the invitation to and inclusion of all of our brothers and sisters, baptized or not, at this table. Through this inclusion, we practice our thanksgiving to God for our inclusion on the basis of God's unilateral act.

What needs to be clear, however, is the costliness of this open table. To say that the table and the covenant on which it is founded are open is not to say that they are cheap or easy. Their costliness to God is evident in their foundation on God's offer of God's self in Jesus. Their costliness to God's children is evident in their demand that we accept them with the repentance of thanksgiving. The fullness of God's love has been offered to

God's lost children through Jesus' invitation to the table. But as we saw in Jesus' encounter with the Pharisees, this offer is also a challenge. When we meet the fullness of God, we are led to a crisis that calls for our conversion.

Eschaton and Crisis

In our previous chapter, we saw that the feast that Jesus celebrated at table was intimately tied to the in-breaking of God's kingdom. It both inaugurated this kingdom of new life, of reconciliation and resurrection, and provided a foretaste of it. In this feast, through our fellowship with Jesus, we have fellowship with God while we await a final blossoming of this fellowship.

The feast of Jesus' table is, in other words, an eschatological event.[16] It is the end. It is the end to which God's covenant with Abraham was directed. It is the end for which humanity was created. It is the end for which Jesus came, died, and was resurrected. It is the end of the fullness of God's love. It is all of these insofar as it is a manifestation of the true end, the presence of the risen Jesus returning in the humble glory of this meal.

The eschatological fullness of this feast is marked by at least three characteristics, which I have discussed above. First, in Jesus' presence, it is the fullness of God's embrace. In this feast and our invitation to it, we find that we have been forgiven, or, more accurately, we find that the forgiveness resting eternally in the heart of God has burst forth to work our resurrection. It is the fullness of the father's welcome of the returning prodigal.

Second, it is the fullness of our fellowship with God. In sitting at table with Jesus, we are welcomed into the circle of God, and we are given an opportunity to take our place within that circle. Here the mutuality of God's embrace comes to fruition, for in fellowship we are able, through thanksgiving, to return God's embrace. This is the fullness of the prodigal's opportunity to accept the father's gift of his restoration as son. It is the fullness for which we were made—to give thanks to God for the grace that God has bestowed on us.

16. Geoffrey Wainwright has explored most fully the nature of the Eucharist as an eschatological event—an aspect of its reality that, for centuries, was lost to the Western Christian tradition (*Eucharist and Eschatology*). Wainwright articulates powerfully the case for opening the Eucharist table on the basis of the eschatological thrust of Jesus' gospel but then oddly negates this argument through an appeal to the significance of baptism and the necessity of only those who have embraced Jesus' kingdom to exhibit this sign of its coming.

Finally, this feast marks the fullness of the family of God, that all are God's children whom God would bring into the circle of God's love. This is where God's covenant with Abraham begins—with the desire of God to bless all the nations. Here we have the opportunity to join with God in extending God's embrace to one another. It is the fullness of the true elder son, who welcomes his lost brother to the table with an open and grateful heart. This is the eschatological end of God's love as realized in the kingdom of Jesus' table fellowship.

We must be wary of this talk of the end, however, if we are to understand the eschatological aspect of this feast aright. We can say that the feast of Jesus' table is the end of God's dealings with God's people, insofar as it fulfills the goal of these dealings—our reconciliation and fellowship with God. But it is too easy to also hear this as the end of our dealings with God—that in this eschatological fulfillment we have reached our goal, that our history has worked itself out to this final salvation. When we make this latter move, we have missed the shock of this ending; we have failed to recognize that God's love in Jesus didn't develop out of our history, but irrupted into it. It is eschatological, because it ends our history, not because it is the end, the goal, of our history.

The practice of opening the table intends to highlight both the fullness and the shock of the eschatological reality of this feast. I have discussed already at length its emphasis on the embrace of God that we receive in this meal and on our thanksgiving as our return of this embrace. Implicit in our discussion has been a commitment to the principle that all persons are God's children, whom God has longed to reconcile to God's self through embrace so that God might receive them into fellowship. This principle allows us to understand the parable of the two sons with the breadth with which it has functioned in our explorations—that all persons are God's prodigal children and not just those with the proper religious affiliation from the beginning. The practice of opening the table, then, is directed toward the fullness of Jesus' feast, but this fullness must be held together with its shock.

The shock is evident in the invitation to the feast through which the table is offered—that, contrary to our usual opinion, we are welcome at this table not on account of anything that we do, but only through God's gracious embrace. It is this shock—the shock of grace—that makes true thanksgiving, true response, possible.

But open table congregations must take care, lest they mute the shock by subsuming the coming of God's kingdom ushered in by Jesus within their own world views and political agendas. This feast is, again, the irruption of God's agenda into a world broken through ours. It is God's meal, through which God breaks down the barriers, not our meal, to which we can invite whomever we please. It is God's project of reconciling the world through Jesus; it is not our project of inclusion through which we are made to feel warm and comfortable.

Indeed, it is Jesus, standing at the center of the feast, who ensures its shock. Jesus not only opens out this eschatological reality into the world but also gives us the signs through which this reality can be known and practiced. The eschatological feast to which Jesus invites us grows out of his costly offer of himself. It is a feast centered in his crucifixion, so that the warmth of the feast is the warmth of his life poured out.

This feast makes sense, moreover, only as it looks forward to his resurrection. We are reminded that we come to this feast in the hope of new life, but not new life that grows naturally out of our own doings—life that we can control and with which we can feel comfortable—but life that bursts forth unexpected from the wild, dangerous ways of God.

Finally, this feast is Jesus' feast only as it includes the truly outcast. The character of the end that Jesus brings is an end where care of the least of these means care of poor, the homeless, the imprisoned, and not just our wealthy neighbors who find themselves alienated from God.

Gordon Lathrop reminds us that we properly celebrate this meal when we not only open our doors with a warm invitation but also are true to the character of the meal to which we invite those who enter.[17] We must maintain the strong symbol of Jesus at the center of the meal in tandem with the open door of the meal so that, together, these can remind us of the shock of the kingdom that Jesus brings. If the meal that we celebrate is not truly eschatological, if it is not Jesus' meal through which God's grace and kingdom interrupt our world, then when we open our tables, we invite participants only into fellowship with our agendas and not into the fullness of fellowship with God.

The recognition of the eschatological element of the eucharistic feast is essential to grasping the dynamic of crisis fundamental to it. As we saw in Luke's Gospel, to sit at table with Jesus is to be brought into a crisis. Jesus' presence inevitably demands a response, and the character of one's

17. Lathrop, *Holy Things,* 128ff.

response defines one's relationship to Jesus and the fellowship with God that he offers. This was true for both Pharisee and tax collector. It was true of the younger brother, whose true crisis occurred not in his degradation, feeding pigs, but in his embrace by the father. It was true, as well, of the older brother, when he was invited to the feast of the younger brother's reconciliation. The feast that Jesus celebrated and about which he preached was a feast of crisis.

The irony in this crisis is that it arises from confrontation with God's fullness. This is why we must remember the eschatological character of the feast—we must be reminded that this fullness is God's, not ours, and that what God offers here is fullness, the end of God's work with God's people.

One name we have given a proper response to the fullness of God thus far is repentance. This is the response that Jesus demanded as he preached his gospel of God's coming kingdom. We can outline the shape of this repentance more fully, given all that we have seen. It involves at least three aspects.

The crisis of God's fullness calls us first to the repentance of thanksgiving. This aspect of our repentance has pervaded our discussion in this chapter—that we were created to give thanks to God; that we have turned from this thanks and used God's world as if it were our own, blinding ourselves to the grace of God within it; that Jesus' offer of himself in this feast presents us with the fullness of God's grace to recall us to thanksgiving; and that what fundamentally discriminates between those who embrace this feast and those who do not is their capacity for thanksgiving for the loving embrace given in the meal.

Beneath this issue of thanksgiving lies a second, critical question. We can receive this feast of God's in-breaking love with thanks only as we are able to set aside our own projects and identities. We will be able to bathe in the fullness of God only when we turn from our histories of working out our own fullness.

This aspect of repentance is evident in the parable of the wedding feast, where those caught up in their own agendas, economic and personal, exclude themselves from the great celebration. It is evident in the response of Levi and Zaccheus, who left behind the self-definition of the profit and power they accrued through their work as government agents out of thanks for Jesus' embrace. It was evident as well in the response of the Pharisees, whose religious identities trapped them into a rejection of Jesus and the fullness that he offered.

This second aspect of repentance, the setting aside of our own projects and identities, is not an arbitrary requirement for the reception of God's fullness. It clears the space for this fullness, while it orients us to God as those whose primary vocation is to receive life from God with thanksgiving, not as those whose vocation is to earn life and expect its reward.

Finally, we find in Jesus' ministry that these somewhat abstract aspects of repentance are brought to a point through our confrontation with those alienated from God and the question of whether we can enter with them into the embrace of God's love. We see this in Jesus' offer of the embrace—his willingness to enter into table fellowship with both sinner and Pharisee, the outcast and the self-righteous. Through this act, he asks us as elder brothers and sisters whether we can embrace as our sibling the prodigal with his dissolution. He asks us, as well, whether we as the prodigal can embrace the elder brother with his judgment and condemnation. He asks us whether we can enter into fellowship with the otherness of our sisters and brothers, even when that otherness challenges at the deepest levels our own self-understanding.

Here we see the intertwining of the three aspects of repentance to which Jesus calls us. We can truly and fully embrace all as our sisters and brothers only when we have set aside our carefully constructed identities, because our identities are challenged by the otherness of the alienated. When we recognize that we share their alienation, then we can receive God's embrace not with any sense of entitlement or resentment, but with thanksgiving.

Opening the table is doubly positioned with respect to the crisis of Jesus' eschatological feast. On the one hand, it is our response, our repentance, in the face of God's eschatological fullness. We open our table to participate in that fullness, recognizing everyone as God's children, as our brothers and sisters to whom we extend Jesus' embrace in the Eucharist. We open our table as a sign that we come here not on the basis of our identities, not even our identity as those who have taken on Jesus' ministry, but rather on the basis of the fullness of God's invitation. We express our thanksgiving for that invitation through our extension of that invitation to all whom we meet.

On the other hand, we open our table to realize this fullness and to confront all those whom we invite to this table with the crisis that this fullness provokes. This table is dangerous.[18] We must take seriously Paul's

---

18. Wainwright is clear that this table is a table both of reconciliation and judgment.

warning to the Corinthians ("Whoever, therefore, eats the bread or drinks the cup of the Lord in an unworthy manner will be answerable for the body and blood of the Lord" [1 Cor 11:37]), even when we don't take it as reason to close our tables.

It is not our job to protect our brothers and sisters from the danger of the love of the God. It is our job to manifest the fullness of that love so that the grace of that fullness might work in the world. We do not see Jesus in the Gospels protecting those who refuse to repent from the crisis provoked by the fullness of his fellowship. God's willingness to risk this danger with God's beloved is an aspect of the mystery of God's love. All that we can know is that to protect others from the danger of life is also to refuse them its opportunity.

To be confronted with the fullness of God's love in the fellowship of Jesus provokes a crisis. The consequence of denying this fullness is simply one's own self-exclusion from the fullness. For the older brother in the parable, this would be a choice to remain trapped in bitterness and refuse to enter the feast. For the younger brother, there's the possibility of remaining lost in dissolution or of being trapped in his own project of self-denigration, proclaiming his unworthiness to feast with the father rather than embracing the father's project of reconciliation through participation in the feast.

Grace and the Relationality of the Human Person

To be confronted with the fullness of God's love in the fellowship of Jesus at table provokes a crisis, but this confrontation also serves as the resource through which this crisis is resolved. In this encounter, we are touched by the power of grace to resurrect and reform within us our essential truth—that we are persons created for God—and this transformative power is generated by the congruence of the relational character of the Eucharist with the relationality at the heart of us.

In the Eucharist, we encounter the character of grace as embrace—the embrace of the son by the father who rushes out to greet him, the embrace of the sinners and outcast by Jesus, who joins them at table. In this embrace, we are awakened to our desire for God and to the consummation of this desire in our fellowship with God through thanksgiving. This is the relational

---

To recognize at this meal the presence of the risen Jesus whom we had crucified is to recognize both the promise and the peril of heeding the invitation to the table. See Wainwright, *Eucharist and Eschatology,* 85–87, 186–87.

character of eucharistic grace. The grace we experience in the Eucharist is the grace of renewed relationship with God through God's renewal of fellowship with us in and through the embrace of Jesus. It is this gracious embrace that transforms us into the true personhood for which God created us.

God created us as persons, and true personhood entails two dimensions that hold within their tension the fullness of our creation. We are, first, created free. Free to act. Free to choose.

This freedom is exhibited in Scripture's beginning in the poor choices made by the first humans. It's also exhibited far too consistently in the poor choices that we make today. Our choices are poor not because we choose this over that—peas over corn for dinner, or a career as a doctor instead of a lawyer. Our poor choice lies in our propensity, again, to choose to define ourselves by our own projects. We choose to craft our own identities, always in comparison to and over against the identities of those around us. We see the truest expression of our freedom in our individuality, and this is a notion of freedom that cuts us off from one another and, more importantly, that belies the truth of our created being.

For if freedom is one truth of our personal being, then relationality is the other. Relationality is our capacity for relationship, but more it is the truth that we are who and what we are only through relationships—relationships that exist whether we choose them or not. We are, and we are who we are only through our relationships, with family, with friends, with a society and a culture, with a history and an environment, and most of all with God. Through these relationships, we are given ourselves. Whatever freedom we have to craft ourselves uniquely functions within the web of the relationships that lie at the core of us.

If this is our truth, freedom and relationality, then true freedom is freedom that embraces the relationships from which we subsist. It is freedom as love. True relationships, likewise, are relationships that uphold us in our freedom—relationships that support, not suppress, our capacity to love and to give and receive ourselves in relationship. To say that we are personal is to say that freedom and relationality lie at the heart of our being, and this means that we find the fullness of our personal being in communion. Communion is the fruition of freedom and relationality. It is the giving and receiving of self in love.

The communion through which we come to fruition as persons is, first, communion with God. Our personhood is grounded in God's being for us that we find in our creation, as God makes space for us and breathes into us God's life, and in our redemption, as God in Jesus offers God's self to us in vulnerability and love. Our personal being is, in this sense, pure gift. It is established not through our own projects—again, our individuality does not make us persons—but by the gracious project of God in our creation and in our restoration in Jesus.

At the same time, this relationality established in God's gift of love comes to its fulfillment as we receive this gift in thanksgiving. Our thanksgiving both opens us to the reality of our personal being—that we are defined by the gift of Another—and consummates this reality in the giving of ourselves inherent in our thankful response. The Eucharist, therefore, expresses the true form of our personal being. At Jesus' table, we receive God's gift of love with thanksgiving and offer ourselves to God in this thanksgiving. The Eucharist is also the goal of our personal being; at this table, in our thankful reception of God's love, we find our true being in communion.

The Eucharist, then, calls us to return to our relational sense of self, especially to the relationship with God that stands at the very heart of us. This relationship, for many spiritual writers, is the essence of our soul. This is the substance of the crisis precipitated by Jesus joining us at table and confronting us with the fullness of God's love. It is a challenge to allow our alienation from our essential relationship to God to be healed and to leave behind the illusion that we are persons insofar as we are for ourselves and define ourselves through our own projects. It is a challenge to accept with thanksgiving the gift of our personal selves from God.

We have fully recognized and realized the loving relationality at the heart of us, however, when we live into the reality that we are grounded in our communion not only with God but also with our neighbor. We must, as a part of our eucharistic repentance, not only receive God's gift of fellowship but also extend that gift to another—to the outcast, lost, and rejected whom we encounter as we come to Jesus' table.

It is too easy for our relationality to be deformed if it is conceived only dyadically, as merely the relationship of one to another. In this condition, our communion can fall prey to the narcissism of lovers, and we are simply for ourselves in a second dimension as we lose ourselves in our beloved. Picture here, if you will, the two young lovers oblivious to the world as they stare into each other's eyes across a candlelit table. This is not true communion; its circle is closed and forbidding, not allowing the welcoming embrace of love to overflow from it. Here, again, Christian understanding of God's triune being opens for us an essential element of who we are.

From the time of Augustine, Christians have understood the relationship of Father and Son as that of Lover and Beloved—a relationship constituted by each giving themselves to the other and receiving that gift of self, in return. The power of this language is evident in our discussion above, as it reveals the essential freedom and relationality—the essential communion—at the heart of God's being and, hence, of ours.

In the reality of God, however, we find another dimension of free relational being revealed, that the love of Father and Son is not dyadically contained, but that it overflows into a third, into the Spirit who is the Love of the Lover and the Beloved. This overflow of divine love is manifest, as well, in God's creative and redemptive work with us, but this overflowing does not begin with God's creation of the world. It is eternally active in the triune life of God.[19] It is an overflowing that reveals the divine life to be fruitful and inclusive, bearing life out of its love and then drawing that life into communion with its love.

This is the true being of loving relationality. It is a loving that reaches out to embrace another, to bring another within the circle of communion. We understand the relationality at the heart of us, then, when we grasp that it is fulfilled not only through our essential relationship with God, through which our personal being is given to us, but also in our relationship with our neighbor, with another, with the alienated and the outcast, through which our personal being comes to fruition.

This returns us to the thoughts on longing with which I began this chapter. The longing that drives the practice of the open table is the longing both for God and for our neighbor. This longing is fulfilled in the Eucharist, where we sit in fellowship with Jesus, who is both God and the outcast. We are true to this fellowship when we recognize, however, that we are among the outcast with Jesus and when we embrace as brother or sister the outcast who stands beside us.

Holy Things for Holy People

We were created for God; we were created for one another. This is the testimony of Scripture from its very first chapters, and this testimony receives

---

19. See, for example, Richard of St. Victor, *Of the Trinity*, Book III.xiv–xv (in *Richard of St. Victor*, 387–89).

its confirmation in the life and ministry of Jesus. Jesus fulfilled our reality in his gift of himself to his brothers and sisters in thanksgiving to his Father, and he called us to join him in both this thanksgiving and this self-gift. The Eucharist is the embodiment of Jesus' gift and Jesus' call. Through the Eucharist, Jesus recreates us into loving, thankful persons who fulfill God's creative intention.

At table with Jesus, we meet God's longing for us; we, in fact, find God's renewal of God's unwavering love for us in the face of our rejection or forgetfulness of this love. Confronted with this love in Christ, we are brought to a crisis—our recreation is not a gentle process. Do we accept this love with thanksgiving? Do we adopt it as our way of being in the world? Do we set aside our own agendas to live within the broader agenda of God's love in Jesus? Meeting God at the table in Jesus, we are brought to a crisis, but in this meeting we are also provided the resources through which this crisis might be resolved. At table, we are not so much confronted by God's love as embraced by it. We are, indeed, surrounded by it through the community of Jesus' body, the church, even as we are filled with it through Jesus' gift of self in the bread and the wine.

God's embrace comes to full fruition in our lives when we return it. To thank God, to love one another, these are intentional acts. They are our embrace of the richness for which God created us, into which Jesus would lead us. They are our adoption of the relationality at the heart of us as a way of life. John Zizioulas calls this adoption our transformation into "ecclesial" beings.[20] It is our movement from persons touched by the grace of Jesus at work in the Eucharist community to being persons of the eucharistic community.

Our existence as ecclesial persons—persons who have made God's loving embrace in Jesus their own—is paradoxical. It is, on the one hand, an act of pure thanksgiving, accepting the love of God as one's defining reality before and apart from any act or response of one's own. It is the reality of the younger son who learns of the prevenient, resurrecting love of the father that restores him to his family after his sojourn in the far country. This existence is, on the other hand, an act of participatory response that returns God's love through thanksgiving and love of our neighbors. It is the reality of the elder son who will only realize the fullness of family membership when he reaches out in love with his father to all of his sisters and brothers.

20. See Zizioulas, *Being As Communion*, 45–69.

Our paradoxical transformation into ecclesial persons is marked, enacted, and celebrated in the Christian practice of baptism. Baptism is not tangential to Jesus' practice of the open table; it is essential. It is the fruition of the love embodied in this practice in our lives. Through baptism, we mark our recognition that we sit at table with Jesus only through the grace of his love—we, indeed, rejoice in this glorious dependence—while we also join Jesus in his table ministry, serving the sisters and brothers who come to table needy for Jesus' love.

Baptism, in this sense, is our intentional entrance into God's covenant of grace, recognizing that the covenant is established entirely at God's initiative but that it courteously allows our participation in it. The covenant to which we join ourselves in baptism enwraps us in the love of God and, through that same love, offers itself as entirely and wholly open. Through our entrance into this covenant, we die to self—to our own agendas and self-constructed identities—so that we might put on Jesus and his outreach to the alienated. It is a covenant fully recognized only when its actualization maintains the full shock of God's grace—that we are welcome into God's fellowship before and apart from anything that we do, and that we are invited to participate in this same welcome to our brothers and sisters. A more complete exploration of our entrance into this covenant through baptism as the fulfillment of the practice of Jesus' open table is the subject of the next chapter.

CHAPTER 4

Baptism and the Spirit

As they move from table to font, newcomers who have known Christ's banquet welcome and his presence before they could prepare or manage it, now undertake to share his work with us, carrying the good news wherever they go, and serving the world as Jesus and his followers have done. Unqualified sinners summoned to Jesus' eucharistic table can respond like Zacchaeus by a change of life through baptism, as the godlike human nature they have from their creation sheds the deadly shackles of sin, and is reborn and empowered with Christ's Spirit. Having seen and shared Christ's banquet sign, in baptism they can put on his new humanity.

—RICHARD FABIAN, "FIRST THE TABLE, THEN THE FONT"

IN MY PARISH, WE have a beautiful hand-crafted wood and steel baptismal font, created by one of our members. It's not particularly large, but it is proportional to our liturgical space. It sits just before the eucharistic table, where the aisle widens at the very front of the pews. To come to the table, you must move a bit either to the left or the right to walk past the font.

Traditional eucharistic logic would place the font before the table as a gate. "We have no access to Christ apart from baptism" would be the claim, or perhaps, "baptism gains us entrance to the kingdom feast." (Actually, this logic would place the font at the door, but the logic is the same.) The practice of the open table, however, challenges this logic. It claims that Jesus sets no barriers to his presence, but rather he openly invites everyone to himself. We simply do not find Jesus erecting fences in the Gospels. We find him tearing them down. With no fence, though, what purpose would baptism serve as a gate?

This last question is dangerous. Those wary of opening the table wonder if its practitioners have any place for baptism. Shouldn't we remove the font from before the table, maybe even banish it from our sanctuary altogether, if it doesn't mark an entrance into fellowship with Jesus? Simply put, no, we shouldn't. If open table congregations reject the image of baptism as a gate, they are rejecting the image of the gate, not the role of baptism in the Christian life. They are arguing for the deeper logic of baptism found throughout Scriptures and the whole of the Christian tradition, a logic that most Christians would readily recognize.

As I explained in my first chapter, baptismal theology is integral to the Christian rite of the open table, but this theology emerges only in relation to the eucharistic theology on which it is centered. It understands baptism as a marker and enactment of our acceptance by Christ at the table and, at the same time, as an initiation into Christ's life and practice at the table. It proclaims that as we enter Christ's life, our life will be turned upside down and we will come to offer ourselves to the world as a concrete sacrament of Christ's life. To enter Christ's church in baptism is to join ourselves to the love that we find at his table.

Within this theological vision, the font standing before our table serves as a call to repentance and fullness of life in Christ. It invites us to immerse ourselves in the paschal mystery into which presence we are invited at table. As we observed in the Gospel stories, Christ's call both preceded and followed his gift of himself when he gathered with sinners at table, but the gift was always central to and generative of any true response to the call. So with our font positioned before the table. For those already baptized, it is a call to remember our baptism and to live more fully into the mystery already enacted. For those not yet baptized, it is an invitation to be engrafted into the fullness of life tasted at the table. In either case, it is a call to repentance and life, and we encounter this call as we approach the table and as we return from it back into the world.

There is a dynamism inherent in the relationship between font and table when they are understood in this way. The table defines the life in which we are immersing ourselves through baptism. It is the life of Jesus' self-gift and of our joining ourselves to that gift, both receiving it and allowing it to define our relationship with the world. But the font will also define our approach and recession from the table. It will remind us that the life we receive at the table is pure gift—that we are born of God into this life and not of ourselves. It will remind us that the life we receive at the table is a life of service, so that whether we are approaching or departing from the table, we do so to serve. It reminds us that the life of the crucified and risen One received at the table is a life that would make us its own—that we truly receive this life only as we are crucified and raised with Christ and that in receiving this life we are truly crucified and raised with Christ. The life we receive at the table makes us anew. Most significantly, though, the font before the table warns us that the Spirit works here, that we dare not approach this table unless we are ready for the Spirit to catch us up.

In this chapter, we will explore the meanings of baptism as it is presented in Scripture's witness, with special attention to how these meanings are refracted through the dynamism of baptism's relationship with the practice of the open table. In the end, we will find that this dynamism is twofold. It is the dynamism of these two rites in their interaction with each other, but even more, it is the dynamism of the love of Christ and the work of the Spirit in which each of these rites find their substance. This latter dynamism reminds us that both baptism and the Eucharist push us to understand them in their mutual relationship to the community of the church in which they are embedded. In the sacramental life of the church, we are led to recognize and live into our reality as ecclesial beings, as persons who find our lives in and through our relationship with God and our neighbor. This is simply a reminder that whatever we say of baptism in this chapter, our understanding will not be well rounded until we have concluded our discussion of the church in the chapter that follows.

Baptism and the Spirit

Mark's Gospel is succinct. That's its genius. Its first chapter is a narrative race from the appearance of John the Baptist through the beginnings of Jesus' ministry. In its brevity, it allots only four verses to Jesus' baptism, but again, that's the genius of the Gospel. Through these four verses, Mark directs our attention to what we need to know of baptism, principally, that it is the work of the Spirit. This is how the baptizer first describes Jesus, that he will baptize with the Holy Spirit. More importantly, it's what we find enacted in Jesus' baptism. The Spirit descends and drives Jesus to his ministry.

The intimate connection between baptism and the Spirit is recognized across the Gospels. Matthew offers a testimony similar to Mark's, but in more detail. Luke develops this testimony further. For Luke, as with Matthew and Mark, the Spirit descends on Jesus at his baptism and drives him out to be tempted, but in Luke alone Jesus returns from his wilderness experience and claims the Spirit. "The Spirit of the Lord is upon me, because he has anointed me to proclaim good news to the poor," he testifies in the synagogue (Luke 4:18).

Notice: Matthew, Mark, and Luke don't simply record the presence of the Spirit at Jesus' baptism. The coming of the Spirit is the point of the baptism and is identified as the active force at the baptism. When Jesus is baptized, the Spirit descends on Jesus and *drives him on*. Jesus in turn both recognizes and proclaims the Spirit as the defining force of his ministry. Whatever else his baptism was to mark, principally it marked the fresh in-breaking of God's Spirit into the world and the inauguration of Jesus' messianic ministry as the fruit of this in-breaking.

Some would refrain from using Jesus' baptism to define the terms of the baptism that we, his followers, practice. Surely our baptism into Jesus is distinct from the theological reality of his baptism. His baptism, after all, inaugurated the ministry through which the way to our baptism was first opened. It's already obvious that I would disagree with that approach.

Soon I'll make a theological argument for reading Jesus' baptism with ours, but for now I'm satisfied to make a simple textual argument. Matthew, Mark, and Luke, together with John, all note the baptizer's distinction of the water baptism that he offers from the Spirit baptism that Jesus will bring, and all four Gospels then immediately note the fulfillment of this prophecy in Jesus' baptism. In Jesus' baptism, the Spirit that Jesus will give reveals itself with power. We first learn about the messianic baptism that Jesus will offer—the messianic baptism to which the baptizer testified—through Jesus' participation in that baptism. This, of course, tells us something about Jesus—that he willingly participates in the reality to which he calls us. Again, we will explore that truth soon enough. But it also tells us something about his baptism—that it is the instrument of the Spirit. According to the Gospels, we only have access to this baptism and Spirit at the conclusion of Jesus' ministry, but equally we must note that by this baptism, the Spirit inaugurates the ministry through which Jesus will pour out the Spirit more broadly into the world.

Luke, at the conclusion of his Gospel, details this transition from Jesus' ministry inaugurated by the Spirit to the fruit of his ministry in his gift of the Spirit. Jesus, having arisen and explained his life, death, and resurrection, instructs his disciples to wait in the city, that he is "sending upon [them] what the Father promised," that they will be "clothed with power from on high" (Luke 24:49). If we recall the beginning of Luke's Gospel and the coming of the Spirit at Jesus' baptism, we should understand Jesus' instructions fully. But if we don't, Luke clarifies Jesus' promise at the beginning of his Gospel's second act.

As the disciples, now apostles, sit gathered in a house in Jerusalem in Acts 2, the Spirit fills the house like the rush of a mighty wind, and the disciples are "baptized" even as Jesus was. Peter soon stands before the people of Jerusalem and proclaims that they, like Jesus, have been anointed by God's spirit—"In the last days it will be, God declares, that I will pour out my Spirit upon all flesh" (Acts 2:17)—and he invites all those who hear to join themselves to this Spirit through baptism.

The essential pattern displayed across these texts is clear. At the heart of the Christian life stands this troika of baptism, Spirit, and ministry. As we follow the story of the church through Acts, we find that the chronological relationship among these elements can vary. Some are baptized, and the Spirit descends on the baptized in response. Others receive the Spirit and are baptized in response. In the case of Jesus' original disciples, if they were baptized, it was at the beginning of Jesus' ministry, while they received his Spirit one book later. We find a similar example in Acts, when the apostles come upon some who had received a baptism for forgiveness, but not the Spirit (Acts 8:14–17). The apostles lay their hands on them, and the Spirit bestows itself.

In Acts, Luke narrates the spread of Jesus' gospel into the world, and the progress of the apostles' mission is marked by the act of baptism and the movement of the Spirit. Again, the chronological relationship of these two activities varies, but the reception of the Spirit emerges as the defining mark of a life overtaken by the gospel. Baptism, in many ways, serves as the fundamental tool of the Spirit's work through which one is integrated into the spiritual life of the gospel, but the measure of a successful conversion is the activity of the Spirit.

This becomes most apparent if we consider Luke's narration of some happenings in and around Ephesus in the eighteenth and nineteenth chapters of Acts. At the beginning of Acts 19, Paul comes upon some "disciples."

Knowing little about them, he asks if they received the Spirit when they were baptized. They admitted no knowledge of the Spirit, having been baptized with "John's baptism." Paul then explains, "John baptized with the baptism of repentance, telling the people to believe in the one who was to come after him, that is Jesus" (Acts 19:4). In response to this very brief gospel proclamation, the disciples are baptized in the name of Jesus; and when Paul lays hands on them, they receive the Spirit.

This passage begins to support the claim that the reception of the Spirit is the goal of entrance into the Christian life both through Paul's initial query about the presence of the Spirit in their lives—this seems the ultimate criterion of the blossoming of the gospel—and through the culmination of the story in their reception of the Spirit, manifest in the evangelical ministry of prophesying, fulfilling the witness of Joel. This support is more evident when this story is held against the one that precedes it.

While Paul is away from Ephesus, two of his colleagues, Prisca and Aquila, encounter Apollos—a traveling preacher who is both "instructed in the Way of the Lord" and "burning with the Spirit" (Acts 18:25). The effect of the Spirit within him is evident in the strength of his ministry. We're told that he preaches the gospel boldly in the synagogue. Luke notes that Apollos knows only the baptism of John, but Prisca and Aquila see no need to baptize him in Jesus' name. In response to the power of his ministry, they only instruct him more fully about Jesus to improve the accuracy of his teaching.

In searching for the discriminating factor that accounts for the need to baptize the latter set of disciples in Jesus' name, but not Apollos, we find that Apollos had a clearer understanding of the gospel, but his understanding was evidently not complete. Prisca and Aquila saw need to offer him further instruction. Luke, instead, directs us through these stories to the work of the Spirit in the lives of the baptized as the measure of integration into Jesus' way. Apollos was burning with the Spirit, and through this fire, he was engaged in the ministry of the gospel. The disciples that Paul encountered, in contrast, did not know the Spirit, and they entered into the Spirit's ministry only after their subsequent baptism.[1]

The early church recognized the essential connection between baptism and the Spirit, and this connection was reflected in their ritualization of a baptismal rite. They established an *ordo* of baptism and Chrismation

---

1. For a broader discussion of these two passages, see Beasley-Murray, *Baptism in the New Testament*, 109–12.

to fully embody the theological reality they experienced in their baptismal initiation into the Christ.[2] As Aidan Kavanaugh explains, "the baptism of Christians was not Johannine, but christic: it was a baptism not of water but of Holy Spirit."[3] In this context, he claims, we understand the water bath of baptism only within the central reality of the new Christian's anointing by the Spirit.

Alexander Schmemann sums up this vision of Christian baptism by describing the culmination of the rite as a "personal Pentecost."[4] Chrismation—our anointing by the Spirit—is organic to the rite of baptism as its fulfillment. Through this anointing, Schmemann explains, the "Spirit gives us Christ, even as Christ has given us the Spirit."[5] This notion captures the dynamic that we saw in the Gospel accounts of Jesus' baptism—that the Spirit inaugurates Jesus' ministry, through which Jesus would pour out the Spirit on God's world. More significantly, it captures a fundamental truth of the Christian practice of baptism and Eucharist that we must observe before we proceed any farther.

My account of the Eucharist in the previous chapter was notably deficient in its omission of the Spirit from the discussion. This was not from neglect of the Spirit, however, but from the conviction that the Spirit's sacramental role is best understood through this conversation about baptism, especially given my claim above that we must understand baptism and Eucharist together. Table and font are inextricably bound.

If we view this sacramental relationship through Schmemann's claim of Christ's and the Spirit's mutual gift of the other, then we first must recognize that the christological reality of the Eucharist is pneumatologically dependent—that the Spirit must give us Jesus. We experience this concretely in our celebration of the Eucharist when we pray for the Spirit to make Jesus present in our midst, even as the Spirit bestowed Jesus on the world, anointing him as Messiah at his baptism. More significantly, perhaps, coming to the table by way of the font reminds us that Jesus offers us an eschatological feast at table in part because his ministry was inaugurated by the outpouring of the Spirit promised by the prophets.

The converse of this last truth is the most significant for us here, however. If Jesus' table ministry is bound up with God's outpouring of the

2. See Bradshaw, *Reconstructing Early Christian Worship*, 85–97.
3. Kavanaugh, *The Shape of Baptism*, 25.
4. Schmemann, *Of the Water and the Spirit*, 78.
5. Ibid., 80.

Spirit, then we should take care not to approach the table unaware that we are moving into the breezeway of the Spirit. The Jesus who invites us to the table is the Jesus who has been anointed with God's Spirit so that he might give us this Spirit. If we dare approach him at his table, we might find ourselves returning his embrace and, entering into his fellowship, receiving the Spirit from him. Approaching Jesus' table, in other words, threatens to make us the locus of the Spirit's activity as we are moved from table to font and immersion into the new life of Jesus.

Likewise, once we've been overtaken by the Spirit, approaching Jesus' table by way of the font reminds us that Jesus calls us and the Spirit empowers us to come to the table to serve. Baptism and anointing with the Spirit are a prelude to ministry; they are our entrance into God's eschatological renovation of the world.

Through baptism, we become loci of the work of the Spirit—of the active power of God. To take baptism seriously is to recognize its intimate connection to the Spirit's work. Baptism was defined by John (the Baptist) as a rite of forgiveness, and forgiveness remains as an aspect of its significance. Through Jesus, however, its focus was shifted. It became an anointing by God's Spirit that puts us in the service of God. This reality shapes our participation in and service at Jesus' table in profound ways, and so we need to explore more completely the meaning of the transformation if we're to understand fully the significance of this sacramental act.

Baptism as New Birth through the Spirit

John's Gospel dwells in paradox. It attempts to express the ways of the Word through whom all things were made to a world that has fallen away from that Word, or even more that has turned its back on the Word. There is a strangeness to God's Word in John's Gospel—a both/and to the way of life that this Word embodies.

Ultimately, John's goal is to push his readers to decision through this paradox. When confronted with the Word, Life, and Light through whom we were made, do we choose this Word, or do we choose to continue to dwell in death and darkness? Baptism is the road taken with this choice. It recognizes that as we come to the table and see this Jesus, so we are left to choose for or against him when we are confronted with his font in our egress. Confrontation with the font, in other words, is the culmination of the crisis that we encounter at table with Jesus, as I discussed in the previous chapter.

And yet, paradoxically in John, the metaphor for the conversion effected by Jesus denies the centrality of our choice. To find life in Jesus is to be born. Born again. Born from above. Born of God. Born of God's Spirit. Through baptism, we are born into the ways of the Word, and we are no more the moving force of this birth than we are of our physical birth into the world. We are by grace the recipients of the natal power of God's love both at our beginning and at our conversion to the ways of Jesus.

John presents us with the paradox of decision and birth at the beginning of his Gospel. "But to all who received the Word," he writes, "who believed in his name, he gave power to become children of God, who were born, not of blood or of the will of the flesh or of the will of man, but of God" (John 1:12–13). The persistent question of the Gospel shines forth so clearly at the front of this statement. Will you receive the Word? Will you believe in Jesus? And yet, embedded within this question is the fundamental reality and cost of this question. To receive and follow the ways of the Word is to give up our own ways, our own agendas. It is to accept being born into a world determined by God's will and not our own. It is to recognize that we are God's creatures.

This dance of grace and decision introduced in the prologue to John's Gospel is explored in more detail in the fabulous story of Jesus and Nicodemus (John 3:1-21). Nicodemus is a Pharisee, a leader of the Jewish people. As a Pharisee, he represents for John one who has defined his life by his own agenda, albeit a religious one, and who is, thus, far from God's Word. And yet Nicodemus is also intrigued by Jesus. He has seen something of life in Jesus—he knows that Jesus "comes from God," he confesses—and so he wants to learn more (John 3:2). Yet Nicodemus comes at night. He does not want to be seen. He is not ready to give up his previous identity. He is in crisis.

Jesus delights in this. (There is a certain ironic mischievousness to John's Jesus. He came to make us squirm.) He pushes Nicodemus with paradox. He recognizes Nicodemus's questions as pretext for his real concern. Nicodemus wants life. He wants God's kingdom. So Jesus offers him that kingdom. Nicodemus only needs to open himself to new birth.

Nicodemus misunderstands Jesus' demand. He misses the realm of the Spirit, and he misses it doubly. His obvious blunder is to mistake the physical for the Spiritual. "How can I climb back into the womb to be born again?" (John 3:4). Jesus illuminates Nicodemus's error. Jesus isn't calling Nicodemus to fleshly birth, but spiritual birth, a birth that we evidently find in baptism. "No one can enter God's Kingdom unless they are born of water and the Spirit" (John 3:5).

Nicodemus's mistake runs deeper than this, though. His problem is not that he misses the realm of the Spirit but that he resists the realm of the Spirit. Nicodemus keeps the conversation in worldly terms because he has some control in the worldly realm. He can still set the agenda here. If the question is new birth, Nicodemus's response is "How can I make that happen?"

Again, Jesus corrects this mistake forthwith. "You should not be surprised at my saying, 'You must be born again.' The wind blows wherever it pleases. You hear its sound, but you cannot tell where it comes from or where it is going. So it is with everyone born of the Spirit" (John 3:7–8). He clarifies that he is truly talking about new birth. Nicodemus has no control. He clarifies more that this is birth of the Spirit. The Spirit is autonomous and inscrutable, and the Spirit controls the reality, the inward grace of this new birth. Or to address our question more directly, the Spirit controls the inward grace of baptism.

Jesus pushes Nicodemus to choose—stop stumbling around at night—but he pushes him to choose a certain abdication of choice. Life, the kingdom—the Spirit's agenda determines these, not our own.

There's a deeper level to the paradoxical reality of John, a reality to which this paradox of grace and choice points us. John's writer clearly lays out this reality, but at the same time, the Gospel never explicitly acknowledges it. This makes our exploration of this deeper level complex. What does it mean to read a theological truth into the Gospel text that the text itself doesn't recognize, even though it provides the essential elements for such a reading? Yet this truth has been foundational to the Christian tradition for the whole of the tradition. In many ways, it served to define the tradition. So we proceed with care.

If the question of John's Gospel is new birth—"Will you be reborn of the Spirit?"—the goal of this birth is that we become children of God. Coming back again to the prologue, John declares that those who receive God's Word "receive the power to become children of God" (John 1:12). John explains the stakes of this game more fully in his eighth chapter, when Jesus distinguishes those who, accepting him, find God to be their Father from the religious leaders who reject him and reveal that their Father is the devil. High stakes, indeed! The question of John's Gospel, throughout, is the question of death or life, darkness or light. Those born of the Spirit move into the light and find God to be their Father. Those who choose darkness are left to its diabolic reality.

But what of the paradox? We need to move back to the initial premise of the Gospel. "In the beginning was the Word, and the Word was with God, and the Word was God, and all things came into being through him" (John 1:1). The premise of the Gospel is that we are all of God; we are born from God. We are all God's own, such that though we did not receive God's Word when the Word came to us, John still claims that the Word was coming to his own. The fundamental paradox of the Gospel is that we are all God's children. Those born of the Spirit are born into a reality that is theirs from the beginning. The power they receive is the power to be who they were created to be. Those who reject the Word have embraced the darkness—have taken the devil as their Father. But even they, in the midst of the darkness, are of the Word. They have rejected their truth for a lie. It's the lie of their own self-determination.

This reading of the Gospel is grounded in the premise of John's Gospel and supported by the emphasis on truth throughout the whole of the Johannine tradition. It's demanded, though, by the whole of the Christian tradition. An initial theological decision of that tradition, in many ways, was defined by Irenaeus—that we all of us are God's children, that all of us are targets for God's grace. The Christian tradition has embraced the truth of Genesis from the beginning. We are all creatures of God and created of God's goodness. We all have no source other than Jesus' Father. We are God's children. So Calvin defines our fall principally as our loss of recognition of God's fatherly love.[6]

Salvation, from this perspective, is not introduction into a new reality, but the restoration of the reality for which we were created. We see this at the close of John, when Jesus appears to his disciples in the upper room. He had promised them throughout the Gospel the gift of his Spirit, and now in his resurrected reality, he bestows this gift. He breathes the Spirit into them, and they are reborn! But we are remiss if we don't recognize in Jesus' action a reprise of our creation in Genesis 2, as God breathes God's breath, God's spirit, into the newly formed lumps of clay, and humankind is born.

To be human is to be inspired by God. To be redeemed by Christ and reborn of the Spirit is to be given new claim on that original inspiration.

6. Calvin, *Institutes of the Christian Religion*, II.vi.1, 341.

This is the truth of our baptism. Through water and the Spirit, we are reborn to our truth. We open ourselves to the claim of God's love that embraces us as God's children. This is the truth of our baptism, and it is revealed most profoundly in Jesus' baptism—but only if we recognize that he shared this baptism with us.

Embracing of Our Status as God's Beloved

In Mark's Gospel, when James and John approach Jesus to ask if they can have places of honor in his royal cabinet, he responds with a simple question. "Can you be baptized with the baptism with which I am baptized?" (Mark 10:38). The implications of this question are weighty and, as we shall see, have everything to do with the mission, ministry, and service to which Jesus calls us. But the question speaks first to our necessary solidarity with Jesus in his ministry. James and John have asked Jesus if they could share in the fruits of his ministry (and we should note their mistaken understanding of those fruits); Jesus' response is that they must first share with him in his ministry as a whole. What, though, does that mean?

James and John ask their question as Jesus and his disciples are approaching Jerusalem and Jesus' passion for love of the world. Ultimately, this passion is the baptism to which we are called. (Again, we will discuss this momentarily.) But we can grasp our share in this baptism only if we understand first how we share in the baptism through which Jesus' ministry was founded. If Jesus asks his disciples to share in his baptism as Mark's story nears the culmination of Jesus' ministry, then we can understand this question only as we recognize that Mark's Gospel is bookended by baptisms in which Jesus asks us to share. There is his "baptism" on the cross, to which this question looks forward. There was first, however, his baptism by John with which the entirety of his ministry began.

As I noted above, for some biblical commentators, Jesus' baptism was a species apart from ours—a unique occurrence that says little or nothing about the theological significance of the Christian sacrament that we share. Their claim is typically twofold. First, our baptism is in the name of Jesus and is a possibility opened to us by the life, death, and resurrection of Jesus. Jesus' baptism by John, almost by definition, shared neither of these characteristics. Second, given our understanding of baptism as a rite transacted for the forgiveness of our sins, surely John's baptism of Jesus does not share this function. Surely, it is a rite apart.

Again, as I argued above, the text of the Gospels offers little to support this claim. However accurate it is to note that Jesus, through his baptism, life, death, and resurrection, opened the way into the reality in which we are baptized, the account in the synoptic Gospels is more concerned with the power behind baptism—both the baptism that Jesus undergoes and that to which he invites us. The Gospels point consistently to baptism as the rite of the Spirit, inaugurated in Jesus and fulfilled in its extension to Jesus' followers. They ask us to see the continuity in these rites, even as they will ask us to see Jesus' call that we continue his ministry, empowered by the Spirit that we receive at baptism.

In making this argument, though, we are given theological pause. Throughout the Christian tradition, baptism is tied fundamentally to the forgiveness of sins. In baptism, Jesus and the Spirit put right what was broken in Adam's fall. If this is the case, though, then how or why does Jesus share in this rite with us? Given the broad Christian claim for Jesus' sinlessness, his baptism does seem a rite apart, since it would have little to do with the forgiveness with which our baptism is bound up.

This isn't a new question. Indeed, it seems to be an original question, as in Matthew's Gospel John the Baptist asks Jesus why he comes to John for baptism. "I need to be baptized by you, and do you come to me?" John asks. "It's proper for us to fulfill all righteousness in this way," is Jesus' reply, and John appears satisfied (Matt 3:13–14). We never have an explanation, though, of the sense of Jesus' response. How does Jesus' baptism fulfill all righteousness? How does Jesus, through this act, define righteousness?

Jesus' baptism, in many ways, points us to the mystery at the heart of baptism. We should expect this, given the gospel claim that in Jesus, Spirit baptism is inaugurated. Thus, we can understand the Christian rite only when we understand its relationship to Jesus in his participation in this rite. His participation in baptism is his foundation of the rite.

In his baptism, Jesus entrusts himself to God. He gives himself over to God. All three Synoptic Gospels indicate this to us clearly. The Spirit who descends on Jesus immediately drives him to the wilderness so that he might be tried and made ready to begin his ministry. In his baptism, then, Jesus gives up any agenda that he holds apart from God's agenda, so that he might be possessed by God's agenda, so that he might embody God's agenda. Note that in speaking this way, Christian theology has always understood that Jesus in his humanity shared with us the full truth of human reality. Jesus, then, in his humanity, was faced with the same question of entrusting himself to God's agenda—of allowing himself to be born of God and led by God's Spirit—that we all face. In his baptism, Jesus offers himself to God. This is the dynamic that we discussed in the previous section.

But equally, we must say that in his baptism, Jesus entrusted himself to God's mercy and love. He offered himself to God in all humility and allowed God to lift him up and proclaim him God's Beloved. He stood not on any righteousness that he possessed apart from God's love. He revealed, instead, that righteousness is this act of trust in God's love. That's how he "fulfills all righteousness." He entrusts himself to the merciful love of his Father.

The logic of Jesus' action is clearer if we consider the alternative. Can we imagine Jesus' striding up to John as John calls the world to repentance, proclaiming his own self-sufficiency, claiming his Sonship, and thanking God that he is not like these others . . . That's the clue, isn't it? Jesus' own teaching directs us to a proper understanding of his baptism. It's not just that he asks us to take a lower place at the table—that we, in humility, should not claim precedence over others. It's more what we find in the Parable of the Pharisee and the Publican (Luke 18:9–14). There Jesus directs us to the righteousness of the publican, who throws himself on God's mercy, and he decries the self-sufficiency of the Pharisee, who rests on a righteousness that he has attempted to procure. Note, Jesus doesn't question the self-assessment of the Pharisee. He was probably a very good man. No, Jesus simply rejects his whole approach.

Jesus in his baptism reveals that the publican's approach, throwing himself on God's mercy—this is not Plan B. It's not the fallback position for those of us too broken to merit God's love on our own. Trusting in God's mercy is the reality for which we were created. It is simply the Plan. It is the fullness of our creation, living into the truth of our relationship with God—a relationship grounded in God's love—recognizing that we have nothing, that we are nothing on our own apart from God.

In baptism, we embrace this plan. We make it our plan, that we are God's beloved not because we have first proven ourselves lovely, but because God is the one who loves. If in baptism we are reborn to the truth of God's eternal love for us—that we are God's children—then equally in baptism, we entrust ourselves to this truth.

It's a strange dynamic of human existence that we are not content to simply trust ourselves to the love of another. We want to earn that love so that we have some control over it. Baptism, as new birth, is a giving up of that control. We not only no longer control the agenda. We no longer control even the fact that we are loved. We simply accept love and entrust ourselves to the agenda of the One who loves us.

So too, having found and embraced God's love in baptism, do we find the forgiveness of our sins. This has been the universal proclamation of the church from its beginning, and it's a proclamation embraced here. But we understand the forgiveness that we find in baptism only when we recognize it as a species of this broader genus of God's love.

That's the only way that we can make sense of baptism, of Jesus' baptism, and really of the whole gospel story. Jesus shares in the baptism with which we are baptized insofar as he immerses himself in the gracious love of God offered there. We share in the baptism with which Jesus is baptized because we equally are immersed in God's love through this rite. Being immersed in this love, we who are fallen find forgiveness. And in choosing to be baptized, in embracing God's love, we embrace God's forgiveness. God's forgiveness is not enacted in baptism. It is not first offered in baptism. God's forgiveness was offered to us once for all in the coming of Jesus. Baptism marks our acceptance of this offer—our making forgiveness our own.

This is what we find when we come to the table with Jesus, whether baptized or not. At table, we are offered God's love and fellowship through Jesus. In our egress from the table, again, we find the font. We are asked if we will accept that love. Will we bathe in that love? Will we let that love define us as God's beloved, before and apart from all that we do? Will we recognize and acknowledge that in that love, we are forgiven?

The prodigal, when he returned to the father, sought at best a partial forgiveness. He looked only for the modicum of forgiveness that he could earn, what his father might give him whether he loved him or not. It's only after he returns, when he is enwrapped in his father's love, that he can find true, full forgiveness. It's only when he recognizes his father's love that he can realize just how far he has fallen—that he rejected that marvelous love and so he rejected his own sonship. It's only when he acknowledges that love—when he accepts it and makes it his own—that he can be not only forgiven, but remade.

When he acknowledges that love, he acknowledges that his deepest truth—that he is the father's beloved—possesses him. He does not possess it. This acknowledgement allows him to serve this truth, to live into it. This is where baptism comes to its full fruition, when through the power of the Spirit and rooted in God's love, we become instruments of that love alongside Jesus. Then we are finally ready to join fully with Jesus in his baptism.

Christ's Call to Serve

Every thread that we have followed in our discussion of baptism pushes us to the conclusion that through baptism, we join ourselves to Jesus in his service and ministry to the world. To be filled with God's Spirit is to be empowered for ministry. To give up our agenda is to give ourselves over to God's agenda of love for the world. To be baptized in Jesus' baptism is to join ourselves to his gift of himself for the world. We saw this dynamic first in our brief exploration of Luke's understanding of baptism as it's depicted in the Acts of the Apostles. There, Spirit, baptism, and ministry are bound up into a single whole. But it's Mark's Gospel that pushes us to recognize the full implications of the fearful decision to which we're called through this rite.

The narrative of Mark's Gospel is bracketed by two baptisms: Jesus' baptism at the Jordan by John and his death on the cross at the hands of us all. If in the first baptism we find Jesus entrusting himself to the loving will of the Father, the course of the narrative leads us to understand the cross as the fruition of God's loving will in Jesus' life. It was to this course that Jesus entrusted himself from the beginning, and much of his energy in the Gospel is spent teaching his followers about the meaning of his commitment.

There is a clear flow in Mark's Gospel. The first half of the Gospel deals with the disciples' gradual recognition that Jesus is God's messiah. Peter finally articulates this truth under Jesus' questioning at Ceasarea Phillipi (Mark 8:29). He quickly learns, however, that he has only half the story. Immediately after Peter's proclamation, Jesus begins the line of teaching that will occupy the second half of the Gospel, that as Messiah he has been sent to serve the world through his offer of himself on the cross.

Peter rejects this idea. He "rebukes" Jesus (Mark 8:32), Mark tells us, and Jesus in turn rebukes Peter. "Get behind me Satan. For you are setting your mind not on divine things but on human things" (Mark 8:33). The reason for Peter's passion is soon evident. He intuitively recognizes what Jesus immediately makes explicit. If Jesus' path leads to the cross, then so too does the path of his followers. "If any want to become my followers, let them deny themselves and take up their cross and follow me," Jesus proclaims (Mark 8:34). In Mark's Gospel, Jesus' teaching repeatedly returns to his destiny of the cross as he journeys to Jerusalem, and at each point along the way he clarifies that this should be the destiny of his disciples as well. This is the context for his question of James and John, "Can you be baptized with the baptism with which I am baptized?" "Can you join me in my gift of myself to the world?" he is asking them.

In some sense, this gift is simply the gift of service, as he quickly clarifies with his disciples. "The Son of Man came not to be served, but to serve," he explains (Mark 10:45). So too they are called to lives of service. This was the service that we saw in a previous chapter, when the disciples had gone on retreat with Jesus. They went to a quiet place but were followed by a crowd. Seeing a shepherdless flock, Jesus put their retreat on hold and called on them to serve the hungry multitude. They were to join Jesus in tending God's people.

If we return to the Parable of the Two Sons, we see this implication of baptism for the elder son alongside the younger son. Baptism is first an offer of God's grace—an effectual sign of our birth as God's children. But it is always at the same time an offer of responsibility—an effectual sign of our engrafting into the work of God's love. Through baptism, we are called to join the Father in his loving search for his lost children—for our lost brothers and sisters. Through baptism, we are called to go out into the world to find the lost and to serve them at table when they return to the Father's house. The baptismal font, then, calls to us not only as we leave the table, but also as we approach it, reminding us that we are to serve God's lost children at this table as an integral part of our participation in the feast laid out for us there.

But the gift of self to which Jesus called his followers in Mark was more than the metaphorical cross of service. The conclusion of the Gospel offers one of the most powerful and insightful passages of Scripture. It is the story of Jesus' resurrection and of the three women coming to the tomb and finding his grave empty. They are met there by a young man who tells them that Jesus is risen—that they are to return to the disciples to report the good news. Instead, however, Mark reports that "they went out and fled from the tomb, for terror and amazement had seized them; and they said nothing to anyone, for they were afraid" (Mark 16:8). Terror and amazement are likely responses for anyone before the miracle of resurrection, but why the fear?

Mark's Gospel, from beginning to end, pushes its readers to grasp the full weight of the good news of Jesus. It testifies to the life that Jesus brings—a life that was fully realized in Jesus' resurrection. But it testifies equally that the path to this life takes one to the cross—a cross that is ours alongside Jesus. With the proclamation of Jesus' resurrection, the young man indicates to the three women that Jesus' path is now fully open. The cross has, indeed, led into life. But if the path is open, then the path is open for them. Jesus' resurrection is an unabashed proclamation of life, but it proclaims a life found in the cross.

This is the path marked by the font at our egress from the table. As we move from our experience of life with Jesus at table, the font reminds us that we can embrace and experience the fullness of that life, that we can move from table to resurrection, from foretaste to the banquet as a whole, but we can embrace and experience this fullness of life only as we embrace the cross as the way of Jesus' life. In baptism, Jesus calls us to join him in a life of service, but more, he calls us to join with him in the paschal mystery.

Paschal Mystery

In his letter to the Galatians, Paul writes that in baptism we have "clothed ourselves with Christ" (Gal 3:27). This terse image captures the mystical reality of baptism. If we come into fellowship with Jesus when we meet him at the table—a fellowship that both invites our transformation and is the fruit of that transformation—then in baptism we own this fellowship; we unite ourselves to it. To Jesus. We clothe ourselves with Jesus so that his reality becomes our reality. This simple recognition renders moot the whole question of whether baptism becomes superfluous with the open table. Only in baptism are we clothed with Christ.

As Paul later clarifies in his Letter to the Romans, to clothe ourselves with Christ is to enter the paschal mystery—the death and resurrection—that he embodies. "Do you not know that all of us who have been baptized into Christ Jesus were baptized into his death? Therefore we have been buried with him by baptism into his death, so that, just as Christ was raised from the dead by the glory of the Father, so we too might walk in newness of life. For if we have been united with him in a death like his, we will certainly be united with him in a resurrection like his" (Rom 6:3–5).

There is something deeply evocative about these images. They capture the fullness of the gospel, the love and power of God manifest in Christ's death and resurrection, and they invite us to share fully in both. This is the truth of the Christian life, and we call it mystery to indicate that we can neither comprehend nor exhaust its richness. Again, it's a mystery embodied in Jesus' life, and in baptism we make this mystery our life. In many ways, this image of being united with Christ's death and resurrection captures all that we've said about baptism. We need to understand that, and for the purposes of this book, we need to understand the particular way that the Christian practice of the open table illuminates the dynamic movement of the image.

To die and live with Christ in baptism is first to accept and embrace Christ's life and death for us. It is to accept that we are broken and that we are loved. Our brokenness is manifest most clearly in Christ's death—that God's love comes to us in Jesus, and we not only reject it but seek to destroy it. In our rejection of Jesus, we see, as well, our rejection of God's love in its many manifestations and our rejection and destruction of one another.

We cannot grasp the meaning of the paschal mystery if we do not see its testimony to our brokenness, but we have missed its meaning if we don't also see its testimony to God's love precisely in the midst of our brokenness. Christ's death reveals love to be God's response to our brokenness, and in his resurrection we see that God's love has the last word. God overcomes and transforms our rejection into embrace.

Our acceptance and embrace of Christ's life and death for us require our own death as well—or more specifically, it requires our death to our own pretensions to life. We must acknowledge that however much we claim life, we actually work death. We must acknowledge our own emptiness, not to leave ourselves bereft but to open us to the truth of God's love. God simply loves us. We must acknowledge our emptiness, then, to get ourselves out of the way of God's love, to make room for it in our lives precisely as love—as something given and not earned.

Likewise, when we have set aside our pretensions to life, we must accept the life that comes from God and accept it precisely as gift. We must die to complacency and self-satisfaction and rise to thanksgiving. Baptism is truly new birth—an action in which we are simply the recipients of life and not in any way the catalysts.

The consequence of an acceptance of our birth, of course, is the death of our agendas as well. It is an acknowledgement, again, that our agenda is empty at best and death—for the world or for our souls—all too often. When we accept that we are born of God, we recognize that our lives are not our own, that life comes from God. So to accept that we are born of God is to accept that we are here to live God's life, to follow God's agenda. We are here to join ourselves to Christ in his gift of himself for the world.

This is the second sense in which we are united to Christ's death and resurrection in baptism. In baptism, we make his life our life, his mission our mission. We join him in his ministry, which is the ministry of giving ourselves to the world. The promise of this mission and ministry, of course, is life abundant. We find the blossoming of love in our lives as we give ourselves to Christ's love. Even more, we find quite simply that we are bound ever more closely to God as we bind ourselves to Christ's life and ministry.

What are the love and the ministry to which we've given ourselves, though? To what have we joined ourselves when we join ourselves to Jesus? Paul, again, summarizes this when he writes the church in Corinth. "So if anyone is in Christ, there is a new creation: everything old has passed away; see, everything has become new! All this is from God, who reconciled us to himself through Christ, and has given us the ministry of reconciliation" (2 Cor 5:17–18). Paul, I think, takes us back to the Parable of the Two Sons.

The goal of Christ's ministry is reconciliation—the renewal of relationship between God and a humanity that has wandered far from God and the renewal of relationship among members of the human family alienated from one another. The goal is the restoration of the lost son through the embrace of the Father, and in baptism we are given the role of the elder son who first searches out his lost sibling and then works with the Father to prepare a welcoming feast. The restoration of the lost son is accomplished when he, through the work of the Spirit within him, calls out, "Abba, Father" (Rom 8:15). The transformation of the elder son is accomplished when he learns to look around him and call out, "Brother and sister."

This is the third sense in which we are joined to Christ's death and resurrection through baptism. In baptism, we are reintegrated into God's family as we're made a member of the body of Christ. So too, in baptism we covenant ourselves to see the dignity of all persons. What is this dignity other than their equal status as God's children? We can see this dignity only as we have died to any claim to a unique status as God's children or, to name the subtle twist we give to this, to a unique status as God's faithful or God's repentant children, or whatever special designation we might give ourselves. In baptism, we die to the arrogance and isolation of the elder brother who sees his love and service to the father both as a burden and as a special seal, and we rise to the life of Christ who sees his love and service to the Father as a gift by which we are drawn more closely to one another.

This is the paschal impulse that drives the practice of the open table. This practice is the embodiment of the paschal mystery. Its goal is our death to our own self-separation from God so that we might live in the love of God, and its enactment depends on our death to our own sense of separation from and superiority over one another, so that we can reach out with Jesus to draw our lost siblings into the loving arms of the Father.

Open Table and Infant Baptism

The baptismal practice of the majority of Christian churches is either richly multivocal or hopelessly muddled. In the previous century, churches that had traditionally focused on the baptism of infants recovered the meaning and practice of adult or believer's baptism. This recovery was occasioned, in part, by the recession of Christendom and with it the assumption that members of a Christian society would be baptized at birth as a matter of course. The recognition of the mission field "at home" as well as abroad awakened churches to the evangelical purposes of baptism. More significantly, however, the twentieth-century Liturgical Renewal brought with it a recovery of early baptismal theologies—theologies that assume the baptism of believing adults to have their greatest sense. In the wake of this renewal, we now find repeatedly in baptismal literature a declaration of adult baptism as the sacramental norm.

The logic of this position is reflected in the theology of baptism that I have developed in the preceding pages. I presume in my understanding of baptism that the one to be baptized is a conscious actor on the stage of the divine drama: one who through the work of the Spirit can be led into ministry; one who can allow God's agenda to replace his own; one who can entrust himself to the love of God, be engrafted into Christ, crucified and raised, and carry out his ministry of reconciliation in the world. The baptism of adults, of those who have chosen to enter into the love they find in Jesus, is in many ways a necessary assumption for the exploration of the manifold grace implicit in this sacrament.

Yet, infant baptism remains the norm for the actual practice of baptism in North American churches most closely tied to the rich liturgical and theological history of the church, at least if you look at the numbers of infants and adults who are baptized in their congregations. It's possible to follow Aidan Kavanaugh's suggestion that we must distinguish a norm from a custom and argue that the practice of baptizing infants is a benign abnormality that has slipped into the liturgical life of the church.[7] This

7. See Kavanaugh, *The Shape of Baptism*, 109ff.

abnormality, while tolerated, should not distract us from the essential theological truths embodied in adult baptism, so Kavanaugh's argument would continue as it neatly marginalizes a practice that has defined the Christian life in the West for more than a millennium.

I don't plan to follow Kavanaugh's logic, however, even though I have assumed the sacramental normativity of adult baptism in what I have written until now. However true it is that a fully developed baptismal theology must be articulated with an eye to its formation of the Christian life of a mature believer, the theological testimony of infant baptism goes to the heart of the gospel, at least as it has been understood in the Christian West. The practice of baptizing infants is grounded in a profound trust in God's prevenient grace and in an overarching conviction about the power of the Christian community's faith, and neither this trust nor this conviction should be dismissed lightly. Indeed, in many ways, the practice of the open table springs from the theological intuition embodied in infant baptism.

So what do we do with these dueling norms from within the Christian tradition? We should acknowledge the muddle inherent in all of our doings but recognize as well the fruitful tension produced by this practical mix. The practices of both infant and believer's baptism are the result of encounters with God that shape our practice and thinking. Both practices work together to express the fullness of the gospel. In infant baptism, we find an emphasis on the prevenient grace of embrace; in believer's baptism, there is an emphasis on the grace of conversion and response. In these two practices, we find the fullness of grace as expressed in the Parable of the Two Sons; but in the parable and in the Christian tradition as a whole, God's prevenient grace, gathering us into the faith of the Christian community, is the foundation upon which any response of ours must be built. This is the insight of infant baptism, and we can understand the relationship of the open table to the church's baptismal practice only if we understand baptism in this, its gracious depth.

Liturgical theologians accurately describe believer's baptism as the normative practice in the first few centuries of the Christian community.[8] Even at the beginning, though, believer's baptism existed in a fruitful tension with the baptism of infants, as we find in the testimony of Hippolytus, "Baptize first the children, and if they can speak for themselves let them do so. Otherwise, let their parents or other relatives speak for them."[9] John

8. Ibid., 35–70.

9. Hippolytus, *The Apostolic Tradition*, 21:4, 33. We see similar testimony in Cyprian

Chrysostom articulates a rich and complex baptismal theology in support of this practice:

> You have seen how numerous are the gifts of baptism. Although many men think that the only gift it confers is the remission of sins, we have counted its honors to the number of ten. It is on account of this that we baptize even infants, although they are sinless, that they may be given the further gifts of sanctification, justice, filial adoption, and inheritance, that they may be brothers and members of Christ, and become the dwelling places for the Spirit.[10]

The sacrament of baptism holds within itself a treasure chest of riches, and the early inclination of the church was to share these riches with everyone within its walls.

Much is made of Augustine's promotion of the practice of infant baptism, and typically when we tell this story, we note his coupling of the practice with a doctrine of original sin. We mistake the evolution of the practice, however, if we don't see that Augustine's interest in original sin is wholly subsumed within his concern for the loving power of God's grace. Augustine, we must remember, is a theologian who is known first for his theological account of his own adult conversion and the catalytic role of God's grace in that process. As Continence reminds him, transformation will come when he entrusts himself to God and does not rely on his own strength.[11] "Prevenient" is the name we have given to the grace that Augustine trusts. It's a grace that comes first and leads us into life with God, a grace that, as Augustine sings, "called, shouted, and broke through my deafness, that flashed, shone, and dispelled my blindness."[12]

This emphasis on grace's prevenience is the central truth captured in the practice of infant baptism. It is a practice that embodies most fully the line of thinking that runs throughout this chapter, that baptism is a birth, a transformation of our being entirely within the hands of God. We give our children to Jesus' baptism in the recognition that they simply are God's children, that they simply are loved by God before and apart from any response they make to that love, that we can and should simply entrust them to God's grace. Our baptism of infants is both the enactment and

---

(*Letters*, 64:2.1, 110).

10. Chrysostom, *Baptismal Instruction,* The Third Instruction, 6, 57.

11. Augustine, *The Confessions,* 199–201.

12. Ibid., 254.

proclamation that we all belong to God from the beginning and that we cannot imagine raising our children outside of that truth. The baptism of infants is the practice testifying to the sufficiency of God's prevenient grace.

As I've stated above, the practice of opening Christ's table to all relies on this truth that we profess in the baptism of infants. It, too, understands that God's grace comes first, that we are God's children before and apart from any response, and that in the fellowship we find at the eucharistic table, God's love shines into our darkness and dispels our blindness. We open the table in response to the truth of God's grace coming first, in the faith that through the practice of the table we can be converted to that grace, even as in baptism we are initiated into it.

We must be quick to note, however, that God's grace is only fully understood within the context of a relationship—that it's the grace of embrace, and true embrace is intended to empower a response. We cannot understand the grace of baptism unless we recognize the potential that it opens for us to respond to God's grace with faith, with trust, with an acceptance and claim of our status as God's beloved.

This, of course, is where the dispute between adult and infant baptism begins and where the second essential testimony of infant baptism can be found. The church baptizes infants only because it profoundly believes the faith of the Christian community to be a real, powerful, and essentially formative force in the life of the believer. We baptize infants in the church not only because we believe that God's grace precedes any response by the one baptized or the community as a whole, but also because we believe the faith of the community to be a true and necessary response to that grace, enabling the growth of grace in the life of those baptized.

Early in Mark's Gospel (Mark 2:1–12), we encounter the iconic story of Jesus healing a paralytic man. In the story, four friends bring a man who cannot walk to Jesus for healing. Because of the great crowds surrounding Jesus, however, the friends who are bringing the man have no approach to Jesus. Not to be deterred, they climb to the roof of the house with their friend, remove a portion of the roof, and lower their friend down into the house to Jesus. Jesus responds first by forgiving the man's sins, and then in answer to questions about his power to forgive, he tells the man to get up and walk as well.

This story is a symbol of baptism for us—of a man lowered down into the house/grave where he is met by the love of God in Jesus and given both forgiveness and life. (You miss the rich symbolism of the story if you don't see the image of the friends lowering their friend from the sunlight into the darkness of the house as a descent into the grave where he is buried . . . with Christ.)

This story is pertinent to our discussion for what it says about faith. In Mark's Gospel, there is a theme of Jesus responding to the faith of an individual with healing and grace, and in the Gospel, he even makes a specific connection between the two when he heals the woman who had a hemorrhage of blood and when he heals Bartimaeus, who was blind (Mark 5:25–34; 10:46–52). Both Bartimaeus and the woman made extraordinary efforts to put themselves in touch with Jesus and his grace, and in both instances Jesus responds, telling them, "Go. Your faith has made you well."

So too, in the story of the paralytic and his friends, the friends go to great effort to bring him to Jesus, to lower him into the darkness from where he receives a new birth of forgiveness and life. Mark then points us to this connection of faith and healing/grace, in this case, pointing us not to the faith of the man who was healed, but to that of his friends—his community. Mark notes that when Jesus became aware of what the friends had done, "he saw *their* faith" and so turned to heal and forgive the man.

The story is an example of the role of faith/response in our relationship to the grace embodied in Jesus, but in this case, the operative faith was that of the community—the faith of those who brought the man and lowered him into relationship with Jesus.

In my initial discussion of baptism, I was clear that the Spirit is the primary actor in this sacrament—that through the power of the Spirit, we are both reborn and empowered for ministry. In the story of the healing of the paralytic, the community of the man "baptized" through faith lowered him into the breezeway of the Spirit so that the Spirit could take him, transform him, and give him new life. This is what we do in the baptism of infants. Again, as we observed at the beginning, there is a variable relationship in the order of baptism and the coming of the Spirit throughout the book of Acts. In the baptism of infants, we respond to the grace of God with faith in that grace, with confidence in the work of the Spirit, and so we lower our children into the breezeway of the Spirit so that their lives, in the coming weeks, months, and years, might be transformed.

So too with the practice of the open table. It is another act of communal faith, as we respond to the grace of God in Jesus—a grace that came first and invited us each to fellowship—we respond to that grace with a faith that impels us to invite any and all to the table to receive that grace.

We, like the friends of the paralytic, bring our friends to the presence of Jesus—we lower them into the breezeway of the Spirit—so that they might be changed. Again, the proximity of the font to the table reminds us of what we are doing when we invite anyone into fellowship with Jesus. We are inviting them to transformation.

Transformation is not a magic act, however. It is grounded and driven by God's grace, it is enacted in baptism, and it is catalyzed by fellowship with Jesus at the table. Nonetheless, it is also a slow and gradual process nurtured by Jesus' community. It's not an accident that those called by Jesus are named disciples. The life to which Jesus calls us is learned, and so from the beginning, the Christian community has paired the transformative act of baptism with the communal response of catechesis, through which those baptized are prepared for and enabled to live fully in the life into which they are born. Catechesis is, in many ways, the substance of that communal faith that forms a necessary response to God's grace in the transformation of lives. We can understand baptism and its grace only as we understand the role of catechesis in the transformative process.

Open Table and the Catechesis of Love

Tertullian writes, "Christians are made, not born." If we attend to the New Testament witness to Jesus' gospel, we find that it both challenges and confirms Tertullian's principle at a deep level. The Gospels, again, are stories about disciples of Jesus—those who are gradually formed in his ways. I noted earlier that this formation is charted across the whole of Mark's Gospel, as disciples are led from an understanding of Jesus, that he is the Messiah, to an understanding of his way, the cross. In a similar but more compact form, we find in John 9 the story of the man born blind who is gradually brought to the point of seeing the truth of Jesus. He experiences a forty-verse catechesis.[13]

So Scripture offers a clear witness to the "making" of Christians throughout its presentation of the gospel, but this witness is embedded in a narrative that is directed everywhere toward new birth. Christians are the work of the Spirit, the gospel proclaims. They are born through the Spirit's imperceptible working, and any contribution of our handiwork to their creation is simply our faithful response to the divine irruption in the midst of our lives.

13. See Martyn, *History and Theology in the Fourth Gospel,* 46–66.

This tension between the making and birth of Christians is captured exquisitely in Jesus' reality as God's Word. Christians, simply put, are created through God's Word. On the one hand, this means that we are people of the Word, to be formed by that Word. Our engagement with the Word enables our gradual transformation, our making into the Word's likeness. I will explore this more fully when I discuss the importance of preaching to the church's mission.

At the same time, from the beginning, Scripture is clear that the Word speaks and we come to be. The gospel is proclaimed, and like Saul on the way to Damascus, we find our lives transformed. This transformation is worked out within us over the course of years, but the conversion at the heart of it can be worked by the Spirit in an instant.

This question of the relationship between our birth and our making is a question of catechesis. Catechesis is the process of making Christians. It is the means employed by the church to guide disciples into the fullness of life to which they have been called. It is not just the proclamation but also the exposition of God's Word so that we may incorporate it fully into ourselves. Moreover, it is a lived reality, not simply an intellectual one. However much it involves conversational teaching, it equally must involve a living engagement with the gospel that transforms our lives in all of their dimensions. In other words, it involves work in a soup kitchen as much as time in a classroom.

In the first few centuries after its formation, the church pointed converts toward a clear order in the transformation of lives. Those who wished to give themselves to Jesus were first entered into the roles of the catechumenate. After a period of not just months but often years, they were allowed to be baptized and then to gather with fellow Christians to first share fellowship with Christ at his table. It was a practice that took seriously the transformation to which life with Jesus calls us, and it gave a clear order and dignity to the church's sacraments. In time this clear order was lost or obscured, and only with the Liturgical Renewal of the twentieth century did liturgical theologians begin to push the church toward its recovery.

The concern had arisen, perhaps rightly so, that the church's initiatory practices were slack. As Aidan Kavanaugh put it, "The danger of baptism being used as a symbol of utter gratuity is that it leads to indiscriminate baptism—with no discernment of whether one really is dead and risen in Christ."[14] Thus, along with the emphasis on adult or believer's baptism as

14. Kavanaugh, *The Shape of Baptism*, 194.

the sacramental norm, substantive and detailed catechetical processes were created to help sufficiently form the lives of those to be baptized so that the faith into which they were baptized would be a living reality for them.

There is a danger, however, in this emphasis on prebaptismal catechesis. It is human nature, as I've pointed out repeatedly, to easily assume a control that belongs to God. It's easy to take a process of transformation that's rooted in the work of the Spirit for our own. When we do so, we may not stifle the Spirit—how do you catch or confine the wind?—but we do constrict the portals of our lives through which the Spirit might freely blow.

Kavanaugh worries about "indiscriminate baptism" that lacks discernment about who is "really dead and risen in Christ," and elsewhere he recommends a multiyear catechumenal process to "gradually ease one into the love of God." Nowhere in the gospel, however, do I find a "gradual easing" into the love of God. I find a love, instead, that crashes down like thunder, leaving those who experience it to long for a process more gradual. Likewise, we find little introspective discernment about the "true" status of a convert's soul. Indeed, in the story of Simon in Acts 8, we have someone who tries to buy power over the Spirit within minutes of his reception of the Spirit, leading to his condemnation, repentance, and growing understanding of the place of prayer in Christian life.

This observation doesn't refute a practice of catechesis preceding baptism, but it does remind us that the New Testament views this catechesis as a lifelong practice. Baptism in Scripture follows immediately upon conversion, and catechesis and discipleship are the continued response of the believer to baptismal grace. They are an intention to immerse oneself ever deeper into the death and resurrection of Jesus. Baptism, within a scriptural framework, entrusts a new believer to the more fully formed faith of the Christian community (as I discussed in the previous section on infant baptism) rather than insisting on the mature formation of faith in the one to be baptized prior to their immersion in Christ's death and resurrection.

Catechesis before baptism, in this vision, serves as a foretaste of the Christian life—with one notable exception. There is a consistent testimony to a catechesis of conversion throughout Scripture—the catechesis that Philip offers to the Ethiopian official of Candace, for example, leading to his conversion and immediate baptism. It was a catechesis that lasted the length of a chariot ride. The catechesis is consistently portrayed as a catechesis of love—of the proclamation and exposition of the gospel. It is no gradual easing into the love of God, but a participation in the abrupt and sudden rush of God's love into our lives.

Infant baptism has its sense in catechesis as a lifelong project for a Christian. In baptism, we are engrafted into Christ's body, and we spend the rest of our lives learning about and growing into that new reality. The practice of the open table shares a similar vision—that we understand grace first by receiving it and then by reflecting on its feel, its power, its texture, and its ramifications for our lives. Neither practice is a rejection of catechesis. Rather, truly practiced, they are both an embrace of catechesis as the journey of life.

From all that I've written thus far, it's clear that proponents of opening Christ's table see the practice as the converting catechesis that we find throughout the Gospels. It's an introduction to Jesus and his love. It's an offer of a concrete experience of that love—again, a foretaste of what is given more fully to those who immerse themselves in it through the waters of baptism. Again, the practice of the open table is fully understood only when we grasp that the practice does not dismiss the role of baptism in the Christian life but understands itself as an evangelical prelude—a foretaste of Christ's love—to the full experience of and immersion in Christ that we experience in baptism.

Baptism, Open Table, and the Communal Nature of the Christian Faith

The whole of this chapter has been grounded on the premise that table and font, Eucharist and baptism, inform one another. The love that we taste at the table, we commit ourselves to through baptism. The love in which we are immersed in baptism, we serve at the table. The interrelation of table and font leads us to recall the conclusion to which we were led in our exposition of the Eucharist in the previous chapter. In and through our experience of Jesus in the Eucharist, we are called to the truth of ourselves. We are persons created for God—to receive ourselves from the love of God and to respond to that love with thanksgiving.

We are created for God, and we are created for one another. The love that we find in God, because it is God's love, necessarily overflows from our relationship with God and leads us to pour ourselves out to one another. The love born in us through communion with Jesus in the Eucharist reaches out to embrace the other—our neighbor—and to bring the other within the circle of communion. In the Eucharist we discover this truth of ourselves, I previously concluded, and in baptism we commit ourselves to it. We adopt as our way of life this love and relationality that lies at the heart of us.

This chapter is an exposition of what this adoption means for us. It serves as such an exposition, however, not because I have deliberately sought to illuminate this conclusion from the previous chapter, but because the reality from which our practices of baptism and Eucharist emerge and to which they speak is a single reality—the reality of the divine life and love—into which we are invited by and through Jesus. Any exposition of baptism and the Eucharist that aren't mutually informing has missed something of the truth of these practices.

The work of the Spirit, we have seen, stands at the center of any baptismal theology. Through the Spirit, God's love becomes concrete in Jesus. Through the Spirit, that love fills and embraces us. Through the Spirit, we are called outside of ourselves and led into ministry—led into a life in which we pour ourselves out for others. Paul captures this central dynamic of the Christian life, explaining that "God's love has been poured into our hearts through the Holy Spirit that has been given to us" (Rom 5:5).

The Spirit's activity in baptism and our decision to give ourselves to this activity transform us into persons who are defined relationally. We are defined, guided, led, impelled now by the indwelling love and reality of God and not by a self-contained personal identity or sense of individuality. Moreover, through this love, we are defined/define ourselves as persons for the other. To be persons filled with the Spirit is to be persons who through our relationship with God give ourselves to relationships with our neighbor.

Insofar as baptism is first the work of the Spirit, we find in baptism that we are born of God. Not that this is a new truth for us—we are born of God from our beginning—but in baptism the rootedness of our reality in God's grace is both renewed and recalled. In giving ourselves to baptism, we embrace our reality as God's beloved. We entrust ourselves to God's love rather than to any love that we win for ourselves. Equally, we entrust ourselves to God's agenda for us, setting aside our personal agendas through which we seek to establish ourselves. Again, in baptism, as we find and embrace our truth as God's beloved, we are called outside ourselves, finding ourselves defined not by our personal projects but by God's project of love.

God's project of love is a project of self-gift. It was initiated in Jesus' gift of himself in his ministry of service and supremely in his acceptance of the cross. It was extended in the Spirit's gift to all whom Christ has called to follow him. It is fulfilled when we live fully into our baptismal promise and give ourselves to the world. The substance of this self-gift is our service to the world, joining Jesus in his life of service. The defining mark of this self-gift, however, is the cross. In baptism, we take up our cross, allowing preoccupation with self to die, so that occupation with the other, with our neighbor, with all in need of our love might live and flourish within us.

This is the heart of the paschal mystery into which we are led through baptism. In joining ourselves to Christ's death—both accepting his love and letting go of our emptiness—we allow self-definition to die so that we might be joined to the new life of his resurrection. This is a life defined by our relationship with God and with God's people.

In my last chapter, I described this as our transformation into ecclesial beings, using John Zizioulas's language. Again, it is our movement from persons touched by the grace of Christ at work in the eucharistic community to being persons of the eucharistic community. The transformation that God effects in us through baptism is both a transformation catalyzed by the grace that we find at Christ's table and a transformation into persons defined by that grace and that table. This should be a central claim of a baptismal theology tied to the practice of the open table. This claim clarifies, moreover, that the eucharistic community, the church, is central to our understanding of baptism as well as the Eucharist.

This is the lacuna within this chapter. The chapter offers a discussion of baptism that omits a fulsome understanding of our entrance into the Christian community through this rite. This omission is intended, however, to lead us into the final chapter of this work—a discussion of the church as it is defined by the rites of baptism and the Eucharist. Given all that we have seen, the church in the context of this theology will need to be relationally conceived and its mission made a servant to this essential relationality. The meaning of this will become clear in the following pages.

Before I turn to this last topic, or set of topics, I want to share a passage from Sara Miles's soul-shaking book, *Take This Bread*. She discusses baptism as she describes the baptism of a six-year-old girl. In her description, she relates elegantly what I've hoped to get at in the previous pages:

> Sasha looked at me, not smiling. "Is this water the water God puts on you to make you safe?" she demanded abruptly, in a strangely formal voice.

I put down my boxes. What was she asking for? Was I being asked to baptize her? My mind raced, flashing back to when I'd stood at the font for my own baptism just a few years ago.

Nothing about the water had made me safe. It had pushed me further out from the certainties and habits of my former life, taken me away from my family, and launched me on this mad and frustrating mission to feed multitudes. It had eroded my identity as an objective journalist and given me an unsettling glimpse of how very little I knew. I was no less flawed or frightened or capable of being hurt than I'd been before my conversion, and now, in addition, I was adrift in this water, yoked together with all kinds of other Christians, many of whom I didn't like or trust.

How could I tell this child that a drop of water could make her safe? I had no idea what Sasha was going through at home, but I suspected it was rough. And baptism, if it signified anything, signified the unavoidable reality of the cross at the heart of Christian faith. It wasn't a magic charm but a reminder of God's presence in the midst of unresolved human pain.

I remembered what Lynn Baird had asked me, when I was contemplating baptism.

"Do you want it?" I asked.

Sasha locked her eyes on me. "Yes," she said. "Yes, I want that water."[15]

---

15. Miles, *Take This Bread*, 236–37.

CHAPTER 5

The Church and Its Mission

A practice of participation which accords with the Lord's Prayer, . . . will encourage a strong center and an open door. It will be based not on the vigorous identification of us as the in-group, but on a vigorous and engaging, holy and hospitable presentation of Scripture, bath, and meal as full of God's mercy, drawing a community freely into their network of meaning.

—GORDON LATHROP, *HOLY PEOPLE*

IN THE FIFTH CHAPTER of Acts, we come upon the strange story of Ananias and Sapphira. It's a story that reflects on our truth as ecclesial persons—that in baptism and the Eucharist, we discover, embrace, and embody the reality that we are persons only as we are from and for the other. We are persons only as we are born of God's love and give ourselves to that love, and so we are persons through our love for one another.

The story of Acts, as I argued in the previous chapter, is concerned with the dynamic interaction of baptism, Spirit, and ministry. But for Luke, it's clear that these are bound up with their embodiment in the church, the Christian community formed by their interaction. The church is the community born of the Spirit, and through it the Spirit is active in the world. It is the community of the baptized, into which new Christians are engrafted through baptism's waters. It is the community that takes up Jesus' ministry, but only because the Spirit has given it to this ministry.

The book of Acts charts the birth, growth, and character of the church, as this is part and parcel of its concern for baptism, Spirit, and ministry. At the end of its fourth chapter, immediately prior to the story of Ananias and Sapphira, Luke describes the church as a community defined by the recognition and realization of the truth that we are to live from and for one another:

> Now the whole group of those who believed was of one heart and soul, and no one claimed private ownership of any possessions, but everything they owned was held in common. . . . There was not a needy person among them, for as many as owned lands or houses sold them and brought the proceeds of what was sold and laid it at the apostles' feet, and it was distributed to each as any had need. (Acts 4:32–35.)

The point of this story is not the superiority of Christian socialism, or even communism—though it does raise interesting questions about the marriage of politics and religion for many on the American political Right. The point, rather, is not only the unity or communion of all those baptized into Jesus but also the manner in which that communion formed their lives. They gave over their personal economic agendas to the agenda that God was working out through this community, and they literally lived for and from one another. This is a simplified illustration or perhaps an icon of what it means for those who believe to be "ecclesial persons," people who are defined not by their distinct individualities, but by their freedom for relationship and the freedom they derive from relationship.

In this context, Luke writes that a married couple, Ananias and Sapphira, sold a piece of land, gave a part of the proceeds to the community, and kept a part back for themselves (Acts 5:1–11). This obviously betrays something of the spirit of the community that Luke has just described, but the real betrayal in the story is Ananias and Sapphira's determination to lie about what they have done. They claimed to give all that they had to the community, not acknowledging what they reserved for themselves. When Peter confronts them with their actions, he avers that their property was theirs to dispose of as they would, but with their false claim, they "lied to the Spirit" (Acts 5:4). For that, the Spirit struck them both dead.

The story is startling, and the retributive justice it displays appears more at home in the early books of the Hebrew Scriptures. We miss the point, however, if we let the dramatic climax of the story distract us from its deeper truth. What is important in the story is not God's vengeance or the church's power to excommunicate the faithless. What's important is the story's revelation of the existential contradiction of Ananias and Sapphira's actions; indeed, the story takes seriously the power of such contradictions to unmake us.

Ananias and Sapphira have, by all accounts, claimed a new identity in Jesus through baptism. They have discovered their rootedness in God's love, and they have committed to embrace this love in thanksgiving, especially through their love of their neighbor. This, again, is what Luke has told us about the community in Acts in the verses immediately preceding their story. Ananias and Sapphira have, by all accounts, claimed their identity as ecclesial persons.

The depth of this truth to their being—that this is their identity both in their creation and in their new creation in baptism—is revealed by the consequences of denying this truth. They make a lie of their being from and for the other, and so they are unmade. They secretly embrace their own agenda under the cloak of God's agenda, and the revelation of their secret destroys them. Being from and for the other is not accidental or peripheral to the Christian life for Luke; it is of its very essence. When you deny the relationality at the heart of you, Ananias and Sapphira discover, you have nothing left.

Two corollaries to the principle of our relationality—that we are from and for the other—are evident in this passage from Acts as well. The first is that our baptismal embrace of the love that we find in the Eucharist necessarily calls us into Christian community. The community is the principal place where we practice our love—where we both receive and give life. That's what Luke tells us at the end of Acts' fourth chapter. "Now the whole group of those who believed were of one heart and soul, and ... everything they owned was held in common" (Acts 4:32). If our reality as persons from and for the other is essential to our identity as humans and as Christians, then so too is our relationship with the church—that is, the Christian community. An understanding of the church is, thus, likewise essential to any discussion of Eucharist and baptism. The community of Christians is the foundation, context, and end of Christian sacramental practices. Hence, this final chapter of our discussion will deal with the church and its mission.

The second corollary to the principle of our relationality points us toward the content of this chapter, that relationality defines the Christian community as well as the human person. Relationality is not just an anthropological truth—a truth of human persons—but also an ecclesiological one—a truth about the church. The essence of the church lies in its relationship to God in Christ through the Holy Spirit, primarily, and in the relationship of Christians to one another, secondarily.

In many ways, this is simply a description of what we find in Acts. Through the power of the Spirit, those converted to God's love by the practice and preaching of the gospel are baptized into Jesus, and so they become of one heart and soul and hold all things in common. This essential relationality of the church defines its mission as well, that it is the locus of Paul's claim that God has "reconciled us to himself through Christ, and has given us the ministry of reconciliation" (2 Cor 5:18).

This relational definition of the church may seem rather obvious. How else would we define the Christian community except through its relationship with God, the relationship of its members with one another, and its mission to extend these relationships to those in the world around them? Yet this definition goes to the heart of the practice of the open table. This eucharistic practice is an extension of a relational understanding of the church and its mission. Equally significant, this relational definition of the church allows those who practice an open table to answer a chief concern around this practice, that it disintegrates the integrity of the church by dissolving the boundaries that allow a community to be a community.

Grace, Eucharist, and Church

I began to explore our intrinsic relationality at the end of the third chapter in my discussion of the theology of the Eucharist. In our encounter with Christ in the Eucharist, we are touched by the power of grace to resurrect and reform within us our essential truth—that we are persons created for God. The grace we encounter there is the grace of embrace, the grace of the father rushing from the doorway of the house to embrace a fallen son, the grace that awakens us to our desire for God and to the consummation of this desire in our fellowship with God through thanksgiving. In the context of the open table, grace is understood less as an infused quality of the soul and more as a renewal of relationship. Grace is relational, even as human persons are in their essence—even as God is in God's eternal mystery.

This relational understanding of grace first became evident to me in the descriptions of the eucharistic liturgy offered by several parishes that practice an open table. Members of these communities placed great emphasis on the practice of circling the altar for the reception of the bread and wine of the Eucharist, and they noted that everyone would remain in their place around the table until the entire group had received. This practice enhances the symbolic nature of the gathering at the table for Christ's meal—that we're gathered in fellowship and not to receive our individual inoculations against the world—but it also makes a statement about the presence of Christ in the Eucharist. Christ, in this practice, is experienced richly and deeply in the community gathered around the meal as an integral part of the partaking of the meal.

For parishes in which the Eucharist is received in this manner, the invitation to communion becomes not simply an invitation to receive the bread and the wine, and Christ with and in them, but an invitation to come stand in the circle of the community to receive Christ with and in them. When asked what it would mean for someone with no understanding of the Eucharist to respond to the invitation for communion, members of these communities answered that one would perceive that someone was coming forward for blessing and the transaction of the sacred. It was clear from these responses that welcome and inclusion into Christian community stand at the heart of this blessing and sacred transaction. In the Eucharist, we invite all into the community of Christ's body, even as Christ has invited us into the community of the Trinity.

This relational understanding of grace is not a simplistic reduction of grace to feeling welcome, however. Rather, open table congregations see the grace of communion as a more complex reality. First, they experience it as the grace of reconciliation. The inclusion in the circle of grace of those who experience themselves as outsiders breaks down the barriers of rejection, fear, failure, and unworthiness that we bear from our sojourn in the far country, the world alienated from God.

The invitation to the Eucharist instigates reconciliation between persons and God, while it can also reconcile persons to the Christian community. Often, those who are most profoundly affected by the invitation are not the unbaptized, but those who have been alienated from the church as a destructively exclusionary and judgmental place. When they hear that all are welcome at the table, they recognize and rejoice at this invitation to receive God's embrace in the context of Christian community.

Second, and perhaps more significantly, the grace of communion is experienced in the practice of the open table as the grace of sanctification. The fundamentally relational quality of human personhood is a theological and not just a psychological or sociological reality, as I've discussed.

Modern individualism, which sacrifices the relationality of communion at the altar of unencumbered freedom, has deformed persons even as it has mistaken true freedom. Invitation to the Eucharist and inclusion in communion, then, offers the opportunity for the remaking of the individual into the "ecclesial person" that lies at the truth of our being. This truth is more fully transacted when one is willing to take steps—baptism and membership in a Christian community—through which this fundamental relationality is integrated more completely into one's being. Opening the table, nonetheless, allows participants a glimmer of what this transformation may look and feel like.

Moreover, the community into which one is invited is not just any community; the invitation to the Eucharist is different from the invitation to proceed to the buffet at the Rotary club, however gracious that latter invitation might be. The communion to which one is invited in the Eucharist is a communion shaped by the paschal, self-giving love of Christ, as I noted in the third chapter. Thus, the community by which one is touched in the Eucharist is such a self-giving community, a reality marked within the liturgy by the specification that we gather at the table in order to empower our ministry in the world. As one member of an open table community noted to me, those who come to our churches are not looking simply for community, but community where they have opportunities to extend themselves in love and service—where they can participate in Christ's paschal mystery. This is the need spoken to, the reality met, when the community offers itself to the stranger in the invitation to come forward and join them around the table where they gather in fellowship with Christ.

We should have, of course, no illusion that a simple invitation would give someone the full experience of inclusion into Christian community, but we can trust that one finds at the table a glimpse and a foretaste of that experience and that this experience could come to fruition when nurtured by the work of the Spirit and the broader reach of the church's life.

Another challenge of this practice is for churches to realize and manifest the relational realities that they practice in the Eucharist in their life as a whole, so that they and those who come to them might be truly transformed. How do we give ourselves to the stranger and invite them to experience with us the relational character of our lives not just for ten minutes at the altar, but in the whole of our community's activity and existence? We'll discuss this further at the end of the chapter when we consider the mission of the church.

This relational understanding of grace also speaks to a particular psychology of desire, a topic broached at the beginning of the third chapter. James Farwell, in a seminal article critiquing the practice of the open table, is concerned, quite rightly, with a culture that seeks to nurture desire through its immediate gratification in order to fuel an ever-growing expansion of the consumerist economy. He fears that opening the table only plays into this dynamic by promising a pseudosatisfaction of the desire for God, rather than nurturing this desire through a catechumenal process that leads to baptism and then to the Eucharist. His base intuition—that "longing and fulfillment are mysteriously woven together in the Christian faith"—is on target, but the next step in his argument—that "the object of our desire is one that transcends our grasp yet gives itself to us, even as our longing deepens"—is a misstep, mistaking the relational character of grace.[1]

The human longing to which the practice of opening the table is directed is not to possess God as an object, nor to possess a quality in the soul. It is not for the possession of an object at all, but is a longing for a subject. It is the desire to enter into a rich web of relationship, with God and one another, through which we are established in our true personhood. It is the longing to step out of the disintegrating ways of the world and to begin to reintegrate ourselves in line with the truth at the heart of us.

If this analysis of desire is correct, then it is pastorally insensitive to withhold the integrating power of the grace of the Eucharist from those who are being continually unmade by the forces of the world. We must recognize that this longing is not quenched by the embrace of God through the Christian community, but is nurtured and sustained so that it might burn brighter and lead one deeper into relationship with the community. To return to the Parable of the Lost Son, the father, on seeing the return of the son, was not a coy lover, teasing out desire through a series of hurdles to be cleared before the son was admitted to the table. Rather, the father resurrected a desire that had died within the son to return to the truth of himself through the embrace of the family within whom his truth lay.

This understanding of grace coheres with a sense of humanity's fall as our alienation from God—our assumption that we are now outside the realm of God's mercy and care. This sense of the fall as alienation does not supplant more complex understandings of sin; there is a full recognition of the sundry ways that we betray the image of God within us as we betray God, self, and other through our intentions and actions. It will claim,

1. Farwell, "Baptism, Eucharist, and the Hospitality of Jesus," 235.

however, that we can begin to be converted from this sin only as our relationship with God's love is restored. Thus, in the theological universe of the open table, the order of conversion, which typically begins with revulsion at our sin and culminates with a turn to God, is reversed—we can truly recognize and repent of our false ways only when we have been embraced by God and have begun to allow ourselves to be transformed by this embrace.

The Body of Christ

Implicit within this relational model of grace is an understanding of the Christian community as the body of Christ, constituted in the Eucharist. The fulcrum on which this understanding turns is Christ's real presence to us in the Eucharist—that in this meal we have fellowship with him, and through this fellowship we are transformed. Christ's presence and fellowship are incarnate in the Eucharistic community, so that we receive Christ in and with one another as we gather together at table. But they are incarnate there not through the virtue of the community—we're far too familiar with the "virtues" of our communities to make that claim—but through the virtue of making Eucharist.

Through this meal, we the community become a symbol of Christ blessed, broken, and shared. We become Christ's body, through which the alienated and broken can experience God's reconciling love. (Note the distinction: In baptism, individuals are engrafted into Christ's body, the church, but it is in the Eucharist that the church as a community is constituted as Christ's body. Baptism, then, engrafts us into the body of Christ constituted by the Eucharist.)

This focus on the transformation of the Christian community in the Eucharist accords with an Eastern Orthodox critique of much of the Western Eucharistic debate from earlier generations. The Western controversy over the what and how of Christ's presence in the bread and wine so focuses Western thought and piety on the Eucharistic elements that the transformation of the community enacted through the liturgy as a whole is often lost.[2] Indeed, in implicit agreement with this Orthodox critique, Richard

---

2. So Alexander Schmemann argues (*For the Life of the World,* 128ff.). This may be an outdated critique of liturgical theology in the West, insofar as the Liturgical Renewal drew a primary inspiration from the Orthodox. Indeed, Schmemann also argues that Western liturgical thinking now serves as a source of liturgical critique for the East, given its fulsome sources. See Schmemann, *On Liturgical Theology,* 15–16.

Hooker sought to reframe the Reformation debate over Christ's real presence precisely through an invocation of this broader transformation and the reality of Christ's presence there.[3]

My approach to the church's transformation differs from an Orthodox approach, however, insofar as it will emphasize the church as the body of Christ that was blessed, broken, and shared in his ministry, much as the elements are blessed, broken, and shared, rather than emphasizing the church's ascension in the Liturgy to Christ in the heavenly realm.

Much of the power of the Orthodox liturgy is its heavenly aspect—its intention to open the church to the glory of the Risen Christ to whom we have been united. But a premise of this book is that we must hold together tightly the risen Christ with the Jesus who ministers in the Gospels, so that the glory of this Christ is the glory of a life offered and a body broken as a means of sharing God's love. My argument, then, is not intended to denude the Eucharist of its heavenly aspect but to argue that we taste heaven most truly and fully when we meet Jesus in his offer of himself at table to us, the broken and outcast.[4]

The church's constitution as Christ's body in the Eucharist is a belief shared broadly in the Eucharistic thinking of many of those who embrace an open table and many of those who do not. But working through the implications of this belief opens up more deeply how proponents of the open table understand Christ's church. The issue that emerges when we follow the logic of the church as the eucharistic body of Christ is one of integrity, and this will have at least two dimensions, as we'll see.

Returning to James Farwell's article, Farwell agrees that Jesus embodied in his ministry the unconditional welcome of God's kingdom. He argues, however, that the logic of participation in the Eucharist, whereby we are nourished as members of Christ's unconditionally welcoming body, demands that only those who have embraced this reality, committing themselves to this welcoming, should participate in it. Allowing those who have not committed themselves to Christ's kingdom vision to participate in the Eucharist belies the integrity of the mission.[5]

Farwell's point carries some persuasive weight, but an ironic implication of his argument leaves the church, in its central and constitutive meal,

---

3. Richard Hooker, *Of the Lawes of Ecclesiasticall Politie*, Book V.67, 338–40.

4. Compare Schemann's understanding of the Eucharist on this point (*The Eucharist*, 27–48) with that of Dix (*The Shape of the Liturgy*, 47–50, 247–55, 263–66).

5. Farwell, "Baptism, Eucharist, and the Hospitality of Jesus," 223–24.

betraying the kingdom's mission of unconditional welcome as a way precisely to highlight and uphold the mission.

For proponents of opening the table, we are most faithful to Christ's kingdom not by keeping the company of its adherents pure, but by embodying in this constitutive act the unconditional welcome through which it is, in part, defined. Indeed, the practice of opening the table is essential to the identity of churches that practice the open table, apart from the welcome that they offer to strangers, for through this practice they constitute themselves as a hospitable and gracious communal body.[6] Kavanaugh argues that in the liturgy, the church is "caught in the act of being most overtly itself."[7] Given the vision of the gracious and welcoming kingdom to which the church is responsible, the church can be itself only as it embodies in its liturgy this welcome. For proponents of the open table, the integrity of the church's mission requires that they embody Christ's welcoming, embracing love in this, their constitutive meal.

We should not neglect Farwell's point that this meal is meant to nourish those who have committed themselves to Christ's mission; and at times, when a church retreats to an isolated and deserted place, it can nurture its struggle to live as a close-knit community. But on Sunday mornings, when we find that a crowd, or just one sheep, has been drawn to our retreat, then with Jesus we must invite them to seat themselves on the grass and feed them with whatever loaves and fishes we have to offer. (See, again, Mark 6:30–44.)

We must recognize that to be Christ's body in the world is to be Christ's broken body, whose boundaries stand open to the outsider. We must be wary of the attempt to define our communion through the clarity of our boundaries, for these inevitably tend to exclude and become, themselves, oppressive. We must remind ourselves that the world against which the church defines itself is not those persons, beloved of God, who stand without us; they are, with us, members of God's family. Rather, the world against which the church defines itself is those forces that serve to oppress

---

6. Farwell (ibid., 235–36) critiques the individualistic bent of opening the table, but the discussion of our working group revealed a practice oriented profoundly around communal understandings of the liturgy and human personhood. Opening the table is essential, from their perspective, to the embrace of God's vision for the world and is an act that seeks to gather the stranger into this vision through Christ's welcoming, communal embrace.

7. Kavanaugh, *On Liturgical Theology*, 75.

and destroy God's beloved. The church as Christ's body is responsible for service to these, our alienated siblings.

Centered Communities

But does this leave the church without any sense of clear boundary and definition? How can a church that will allow all to enter and participate provide itself a sense of integrity that will enable communal life to thrive? Here we come across one of the most interesting insights born from the practice of the open table—that the community of Christ's body has integrity in the midst of these open boundaries because it is defined and held together not by its boundaries, but by its bonds. It is the commitment and connection of the members of the church to the heart of the church—Christ's embracing love—and to each other that holds the church together.

Members of open table congregations can be quite clear about the identities of the communities to which they belong, and they typically feel no threat of disintegration of those communities through their practices of inclusion. Their identities are bound to the love of God that they feel is active and manifest in sundry ways in their communities; indeed, it is this love that brought them to these communities in the first place.

The dynamism of this active love, moving from the center of the church—Christ's presence in the Eucharist—and enwrapping all of the church's members, holds these Christian communities together. From this perspective, the inclusionary embrace of the open table in no way threatens the church's identity; it affirms and supports it as yet another practice of Christ's embracing love.[8]

Notice the important conceptual shift that we are making here. Within much of the sociological literature of the twentieth century, the idea of "community" was in many ways defined by the idea of "boundary." Anthony Cohen writes, "By definition, boundary marks the beginning and end of the community."[9] By definition, the boundary defines the community.

Cohen's logic begins with an idea of community that involves a similarity among its members and a difference from everyone else. The boundary marks this similarity and difference. These distinctions are vital to a

---

8. Gordon Lathrop speaks consistently of a Christian community as a place with strong symbols at the center and open doors. (See Lathrop, *Holy Things*, 132ff.; *Holy People*, 93ff.)

9. Cohen, *The Symbolic Construction of Community*, 12.

sense of community for Cohen, so that when they are lost, boundaries "become anomalous and the integrity of the 'community' that they enclose has been severely impugned."[10]

Concerns about the effect of opening the table on Christian community often trade on the connection between community and boundary. Farwell will claim that boundaries are essential for communal definition and identity. Without boundaries, he worries, it is difficult if not impossible for someone to gain a sense of belonging to a community, and even more for them to negotiate real belonging. Indeed, Farwell insists that concern for boundaries isn't a theological position but simply a sociological or anthropological one; and again, much of the literature from the twentieth century would bear him out.

The pervasiveness of this connection between boundaries and community is evident when we recognize it functioning in authors whose commitments seem very much in line with those I've outlined in this text. Serene Jones, in her fascinating book *Feminist Theory and Christian Theology*, addresses a theology of the church in her last chapter, and there she wants to evoke a church that has both a clear identity and a bold freedom to love those outside itself. The metaphor she chooses is "bounded openness."[11]

For Jones, boundaries are essential to the church. They provide it "defined edges" and the resilient and substantive identity it requires in order to be truly open to those on the outside. Jones's vision is of a church "forever transgressing its boundaries," but the boundaries, for her, are the foundation for this transgression.

Is this right? Are boundaries essential, even primary, for conceptualizing community, or is there another direction that we could take? Jones, interestingly enough, provides a way out of this bounded box. Even as she argues that Christian practices provide the Church the *boundaries* necessary for a well-formed identity, she also alludes to the power of the church's practices to *bind* us one to another, and presumably also to God in Christ. It's a subtle shift, from bounds to bonds, but it can radically reorient our conceptual universe and, with it, our understanding of the church.

---

10. Ibid., 20.

11. Jones, *Feminist Theory and Christian Theology*, 167–76.

Bonds, Not Boundaries

If the concept of boundaries was closely tied to the idea of community in the twentieth century, in the first decade of this twenty-first century, more attention has been paid to the role of relationships in community (sometimes under the vocabulary of networks or social capital). This shift forms the substance of Robert Putnam's epochal work *Bowling Alone*, which traces the breakdown in contemporary community in tandem with the dissolution of those relationships that make community possible.

Putnam and much contemporary literature cannot assume a world where the potency of community allows a sociologist to consider only the question of differentiating one community from another. Rather, as the very reality of community has come under fire in our atomizing world, writers have turned to the substance of true community, the relationships from which it is formed, to conceptualize its essential qualities.

Zygmunt Bauman, in fact, derides the connection between the idea of community and the fact of boundaries, arguing that "community" is invoked only to give symbolic substance to the boundaries we erect in our never-ending war to protect "us" from "them."[12] Bauman suggests that the hope of a way forward out of our boundary-drawing quagmire is in authentic relationships that truly recognize the other—relationships from which real community and real security could be derived.[13]

The practice of the open table relies on an idea of community defined by its bonds, its relationships, not its boundaries. In one sense, this is again to say that it's a theology bound up with our practice of the church's liturgy. As Gordon Lathrop has argued, good liturgy begins with strong symbols (of Jesus) in the center—symbols that bind us to God's love in and through the Jesus they manifest. Relying on these symbols, good liturgy also necessitates open doors (a lowered sense of boundaries) since we betray the very symbols that center us if we fence them off in order to define and protect "us" from "them."[14]

To return to an idea from the third chapter, the practice of the open table entails a covenantal theology, recognizing that covenant is primarily about relationship—first our relationship with God and, through that, our relationship with one another. The covenant enacted in Jesus, however,

12. Bauman, *Community.* See especially 7–20.
13. Ibid., 124–43.
14. Lathrop, *Holy Things*, 121ff.

is fundamentally an open covenant—a covenant intended to break down boundaries, which compels us to reach out to the "them" outside of our communities, imploring them to recognize their status with us as God's children. In this context, an idea of boundaries is not only inessential to the reality of Christ's covenant—it in fact betrays it.

Farwell is probably correct that clear boundaries facilitate a clean entrance into a community, but this seems to be a lazy way to do community. A church can be defined by the walls that surround it, or by the table that it houses. The nice thing about walls is that once they are built, they need little attention as they divide the inside from the outside. So too, with sturdy walls, we only need to make sure that we are inside the doors to "belong." This, unfortunately, describes too many members of our churches—both those who practice an open table and those who do not. But if the church is defined by its table, then the table requires constant attention for the church to truly subsist. The table must be set, people seated and served, fellowship engaged in. Entrance into this community can be equally clear. It begins with an invitation to be seated and culminates (in baptism) with an invitation into the kitchen to join those who serve.

All of this is not to deny the role of boundaries in the Christian community, however. It's only to recognize that they are there not to hold us together or give us identity; rather, they serve to protect us, not from the "them" whom they fence out, but from the forces that oppress us and that oppress "them." We require safety not from the unbaptized, but from the destructive forces in the world that would invade our hearts. The Other from which the church must distinguish itself in our world is the force of oppression, exclusion, and degradation that threatens to unmake us. Those who are not baptized are those who need the church's protection, seeking safe haven among us. The practice of open table is one bulwark through which the church provides them passage into port.

The People of God

The church as the body of Christ is one image, then, that begins to capture the church's relational nature. It's an image that's eucharistically centered— we become Christ's body through our fellowship with him in the Eucharist. It's also an image that is outward looking. To call ourselves Christ's body is to recognize that we have been joined to Christ so that we might offer ourselves with him to a broken world. It reminds us that in baptism, in joining ourselves to Christ, we join ourselves to his paschal gift of himself to the world.

There's a second image of the church, the church as the people of God, that picks up on a relational understanding of the church and that, paradoxically, leads us more deeply into an understanding of the church's intimate relationship with the world. This latter point is paradoxical only because this image of the church has traditionally conveyed more the disconnection between the church and the world. But when the image is seen in the context of the practice of the open table, it is transformed to pick up more fully the broader biblical narrative of which it is a part.

In his lovely book *The Churches the Apostles Left Behind*, Raymond Brown explores with his readers the variety of ecclesiological models and images that we find throughout the various traditions collected into the New Testament.[15] In each section, he describes a community to which a book or selection of books in the New Testament seems to be addressed, looks at the images of the church offered to each of these communities, and then assesses the strengths and weaknesses of each tradition.

When he turns to the tradition captured in 1 Peter, he first describes for us the prospective audience of the letter: "To the chosen exiles of the diaspora in Pontus, Galatia, Cappadocia, Asia, and Bithynia" (1 Pet 1:1). Brown surmises that the letter was written to a scattering of small Christian communities in the northern parts of Asia Minor (the area that is now Turkey)—communities of Gentiles who were distant from the Christian community as a whole. They were surrounded by a pagan culture that in turns distrusted, disdained, and at times persecuted them. They were, by Brown's analysis, a set of communities beset with a sense of alienation and ostracism, in need of connection and belonging.[16]

In response, Brown argues, the author of 1 Peter offers these communities encouragement and a vision of their lives embedded in the narrative of the Hebrew Scriptures. He asks them to see themselves in the stories of Israel's exodus from Egypt, its wanderings in the desert, and its deliverance into the promised land. He reminds them that they once were "no people," but that now they are "God's people" (drawing on the language of the prophet Hosea), that they, "like living stones, are being built into a spiritual house to be a holy priesthood, to offer spiritual sacrifices to God through Jesus Christ" (1 Peter 2:5).

15. Brown, *The Churches the Apostles Left Behind*.
16. Ibid., 78–79.

First Peter, Brown argues, "counteracted this alienation [experienced by these isolated communities] by the assurance that in Christianity, Gentile converts had found a new family, a new home, a new status that made them a special people with an imperishable inheritance."[17] It gave them a story, but more significantly, it made them a part of God's story. It accentuated their status in God's eyes, giving a real significance to their lives.[18] They not only belonged. They were a people about something.

There is danger, of course, in this kind of imagery, designating the Christian community as the people of God. There is, as Brown puts it, "a sense of exclusive eliteness inherent in designating any group as belonging more closely to God."[19] It can breed a certain arrogance or a sectarian isolationism. It does little to allow a community to connect to the world around it, and from everything we've seen in this book thus far, it would seem to betray the embracing love of God that Jesus represented.

But is that necessarily the case? The "people of God" is a powerful image, but it seems to me that it's only an exclusionary image if you read it exclusively. The trick, as Augustine might say, is learning to read passages like this through the lens of the love of God. In this book, that has meant in the first place to read it through the lens of the Parable of the Two Sons.

What's striking when we consider the image of the people of God is the deep sense of connection or relationship that lies at its heart. To be God's people is to belong to God. To pick up the language of the parable, it's to be reminded by the father that "you are always with me, and all that I have is yours" (Luke 15:31). Again, there's the possibility of exclusivity there, but mostly there is the reality of belonging and the reminder that this belonging to God constitutes our chief riches. That's the lesson of the parable—that the elder son is selling out cheaply if his goal is the fatted calf. The greater riches are found in the father's unfailing presence.

But if we read this imagery from Peter through the lens of the parable, we're reminded of two more things as well, each of which challenges any sense of exclusivity that the image may suggest. First, we must remember that when the father in the parable instructs his son, "all that is mine is yours"—the first and greatest possession of the father is his love for his children and, more specifically, for his alienated son.

17. Ibid., 79.

18. For more on status inconsistency, see Meeks, *The First Urban Christians*, 22ff.

19. Brown, *The Churches the Apostles Left Behind*, 81.

This love for the alienated belongs to the elder son as well, and it belongs to him as a privilege and a treasure. To be God's people means to share in God's mission in the world—to share in God's reconciliation with the world. When 1 Peter exhorts his communities that they, "like living stones, are being built into a spiritual house to be a holy priesthood," we must remember that their priestly mission is to reconcile an alienated world to God. They are built as a spiritual house so that their doors might be open and the world served at Christ's table within.

Second and implicit in this last point, the Parable of the Lost Son reminds us that those outside of our community are equally God's children, equally God's people. This intuition—that all are God's children whom God longs for and seeks—is essential to the practice of the Christian life in so many open table congregations.

This intuition is twofold. It is a recognition that those "outside" our communities have full claim to God's love and to our love—hence their inclusion at the meal. More fundamentally, though, it's a recognition and acknowledgement that our claim to God's love is the same as theirs. We all are God's alienated children, we all have drifted from God's love, and we all have standing in God's house on the basis of God's extravagant grace.

Notice that I didn't write that we have standing "only" on the basis of God's grace. An "only" here would imply that there is some other possible standing before God, some higher standing for which we could strive if we were only better. Again, as I argued in the previous chapter, grace is not the default option. It is the full fruition of God's love in our lives. All of God's creation, all of God's children have standing on the basis of grace. All are God's people in and through God's grace. When the church takes up the imagery of the "people of God," it simply claims the grace of which we are all heirs, in hopes of offering it to our brothers and sisters, but ever mindful that we must also be open to receiving this grace from them. It is theirs as much as it is ours.

Spirit, Church, and World

When we understand in this way the church in relation to this image of the people of God, we have located the church at a particular nexus in the biblical story—a vital nexus, if not *the* vital nexus in understanding God's relationship with God's creation. We've located it at a place that asks the church to recognize its similarity with the world at its deepest level—that we are all God's people, God's children, the objects of God's gracious love. We've at the same time located the church at a place that notes its difference from the world (understanding the world as humanity [all of us] in our alienation from God), that the church is that community that makes a claim with faith and thanksgiving on its status as God's people, a status, again, that we share with the world, but from which the world is alienated. From this similarity and difference, we've established a relationship between church and world—that God has called a church both to stand in solidarity with the world and to reconcile the world to God. God has given us a ministry of reconciliation.

We have located the church, the world, and their relationship with each other, in other words, at the beginning of the biblical story, as Genesis moves from its eleventh to its twelfth chapter and beyond. We've located it at the turning point in the biblical narrative, when the tower of Babel and humanity's alienation from God and from each other lead God to the calling of Abraham and in him a people to be a blessing to the nations. I introduced this idea in the third chapter's discussion of the covenant sealed by Jesus. What we see in Genesis 12 is God's calling of a true elder sibling, Abraham and his descendents, to be a people through which God pursues a prodigal world that has disintegrated through its hubris and its blindness to grace.

To say that we have located the church here at this turn in the biblical narrative is to follow Calvin in his understanding of the church and God's story with the world. Calvin argues that in God's calling of Abraham, we see the birth of the church.[20] It's the birth of a redemptive people with whom God would work out God's salvation. (Let me be quick to note, with Calvin, that God works out God's salvation with this people more often through their faithlessness and alienation from God than through any virtue they display. There is no triumphalism in this vision of the church.)

Calvin's view complements the traditional understanding that the church was born in the second chapter of Acts, when God pours out God's spirit on the gathered Christian community. What we see in the Pentecost moment is the fruition of what God began in Abraham in response to the disintegration of Babel. On Pentecost, God reaches out to a fragmented world through the community gathered by Christ's Spirit, speaking to everyone in their own language of the reality of God's welcoming love.

---

20. Calvin, *Commentaries on the Book of Genesis,* vol. I, 343.

Locating the church here in these twin moments reminds us, first, that God has called the church for mission, or, more specifically, for the mission of reconciling the world to God. I have said this repeatedly, but I find it helpful to attach this idea to a story—the world's biography, if you will. It's a story that reminds us not only that the church has an intimate relation with the world but also that the world's alienation is the reason for which God has called the church. And we must remember that we have a full share in that alienation. Just as we all stand before God as the lost son who is only coming to understand the full meaning of the Father's embrace, so too we have a full share in Babel's disintegration. The brokenness and division of Babel are as evident within the church as without it. These divisions, ironically, help to solidify the solidarity of the church with the world.

If the reality of the church is relational, then surely that must involve the church's relationship with the world—with our sisters and brothers outside the church—as well as its relationship to Jesus at the center of its community and the relationships of its members to one another. The church exists as the community of those in fellowship with Jesus—those who have been baptized into his death and resurrection. But with Jesus, the church exists as a community to serve the world, recognizing that our service is grounded in our solidarity with the world, that we are all brothers and sisters.

Locating the birth of the church between the bookends of Babel and Pentecost reminds us, first, that the church is called for mission, and second, therefore, that the church is a Pentecostal reality. However much the church is shaped by the reality of Jesus at its center, it is equally shaped and guided by the reality of God's Spirit that blows through it. This is what empowers open table congregations to invite all to fellowship with Jesus. They do so in the conviction that at the table, in the midst of the church, we all stand in the breezeway of the Spirit.

The Eucharist has been called an instrument of Christian unity, not simply testifying to unity but creating it. This can refer us to the unity within the Christian community. Through our participation in Christ's meal, we are united to one another as we join in fellowship with Jesus.

But from what we have seen, God's principal concern in calling a church is the reconciliation of a broken humanity with God and with one another. If the Eucharist is God's instrument, then it must be instrumental in this reconciling process. If it's an instrument of unity, then it must be significantly focused on reuniting God's alienated children to their loving, searching Father. This is the practice of open table congregations. They bring God's children to Christ's table, and so they bring them to the Spirit's breezeway and the possibility of reconciliation with God.

The Mission of the Church

The reflections of this book began with the claim in the first chapter that "opening the table is a rite and not a rubric, that it is a whole style of Christian living through which the redeemed world is done and not merely a simple invitation that we offer on Sunday morning." All that has followed develops the substance of that claim. It fleshes out the style of Christian living in which this practice finds its home. Practitioners of the open table are only true to this "rite" if they strive to embody fully in their life rudiments of this style. They are called to Christ's ministry of reconciliation in particular ways.

I have throughout this text been wary of equating the practice of the open table with the virtue of hospitality only because for too many hospitality means "mere" hospitality—what we can learn from magazines about proper manners and entertaining guests. But when we recognize that hospitality is a cardinal virtue within the biblical story, then perhaps we can frame the practice of the open table more appropriately.

We again must remember first that the church was born of Abraham because of his hospitality—that he "entertained angels unawares" (Heb 13:2). We must be mindful that the simple hospitable act of an innkeeper, making space in the stable for a wandering family when there was no room in the main building, allowed the body of Christ to be born into the world. In both of these examples, space was made for grace in a world for which grace was anathema.

What's apparent when we recall these stories is that hospitality, if it is truly hospitality, cannot stand as a simple "symbolic" act—an act devoid of substance, sincerity, or follow-through. Hospitality, to use our liturgical language, cannot be a mere set of rubrics but must be a whole style of living. It must encompass the whole of our lives. When hospitality is understood in this fulsome way, it becomes an appropriate metaphor for articulating the church's mission of reconciliation. Hospitality not only creates space for relationship; it also invites and nurtures it. We can explore the church's mission more fully if we consider what it would mean for the church to be truly hospitable.

This will involve, at the least, thinking through three aspects of the church's hospitality: its evangelical aspects—how we are truly hospitable only as we offer the fullness of the gospel to those who come to our tables hungry; its catechetical aspects—how we are truly hospitable only as we help people to move from the table to the kitchen, to become, in other words, truly a part of our communal families; and its diaconal aspects—that we neglect true hospitality if we think that we can separate the so-called spiritual needs of those who would come to our tables from the physical or social needs. Let's look at each of these in turn.

Evangelical Hospitality

In the story of the wedding feast at Cana in Galilee, the steward of the feast indirectly compliments Jesus for serving the best wine. Implicit in this compliment is the assumption that the hospitable host serves the best wine. This is the first and clearest challenge for parishes that open their table—that we serve the best wine.

We must be clear that however much the people who come through our doors desire community or purpose or fellowship or a sense of belonging, the food that they truly long for is God, Jesus, the Spirit. They may not be able to name this desire. They may not even know that this hunger lies within them, but this is the best wine, the main course that we have to offer. We must not only offer it, but we must offer it clearly and fully. We must name the dish, not for fear that they are allergic to it—though some may be and may refuse to dine with us on that account—but out of the conviction that if they can attend to the taste of grace, they will return to the table to taste it again and again.

This recalls, again, Gordon Lathrop's assertion that liturgical acts are true when they maintain strong symbols at their center. The symbol itself will change hearts if it is only allowed to resonate. A member of St. Mark's Episcopal Church in Washington, DC, once confided in me that he began attending the church out of an intellectual curiosity married to a vague spiritual longing. (St. Mark's had for several decades advertised itself as a church for "skeptics and believers alike.") He attended, in other words, for the sermons and conversations around them. The rest of the service, particularly the table, was simply motions to occupy the remaining time for him. After more than a decade of attendance and participation, though, the table had changed him. He had a defined, not a vague, spirituality, and it was defined by the bread and the wine and the reception of Jesus in them. The symbol did the work. The church only needed to allow it to speak.

When we open our tables, we must be clear that it is Jesus' table to which we are all invited, that we have fellowship with him there, that he is present. We must name the table and the presence in our prayers, but we also need to name the table in our invitation. Again, some may be allergic to that naming, but it is only fair to them to identify clearly what we are offering. We should never try to covertly slip someone a little Jesus.

We must be equally clear that the Spirit is dangerously present here, that lives can be changed if we aren't careful. In part, this can mean that we name the Spirit in our invitation and prayers. More importantly, though, we need to believe in the work of the Spirit. We need to make time and space for the Spirit to blow. Is there room in our liturgy around the table for people to speak of the Spirit's movement in their lives? Is there room for people to open themselves to the Spirit's healing through prayer and the laying on of hands?

An openness to the Spirit around our table is most evident in the expectation that we bring to the table. Thomas Merton, in his story of his conversion, tells of his first trip to the monastery at Gethsemane, Kentucky, for retreat. When Merton entered the monastery, the gatekeeper asked him if he had come there to stay. Merton was startled, and frightened a bit; yet this expectation worked in his heart. On his next trip to Gethsemane, when the gatekeeper asked if this time he would stay, he could respond, "Yes, Brother, if you'll pray for me."[21]

We can express a sense of expectation around the table in numerous ways. One priest, in his invitation to the table, reminds all those present that when they come forward, they will partake of both gifts and a responsibility—they are invited, in other words, always to the fullness of grace. Another priest, in her invitation, proclaims, "Wherever you are in your journey—whoever wants to meet Jesus, come to the table."

We practice this expectant hospitality most fully, however, when it is found not just in the invitation offered by the priest, but in the welcome extended by the community as a whole. When we greet those who have joined us at the table with the question, "Have you come here to stay?" or when we orient them to our community with the expectation that they will want to stay, then we have recognized that the fullness of what we have to offer lies not in the simple reception of the Eucharist, but in the embrace

21. Merton, *The Seven Storey Mountain*, 408.

of the Christian community and the gospel way of life to which it is called. Only with this recognition have we truly opened our tables, our lives, and God's world to those who come into our midst. Only thus have we made hospitality a way of life.

Catechetical Hospitality

All that we say about the evangelical character of our hospitality at the table entails, as well, a catechetical imperative. The goal of our hospitality is not simply to make someone feel like a welcome guest, but to provide a means by which they might become a member of the family. Indeed, as we saw above, we offer our hospitality always with the hope and expectation that those we invite to the table might not only meet Jesus, but join themselves to him, and so to us, his family. We hope that they will come to serve at the table and not just feast at it. A truly hospitable table, therefore, will attend not only to the good news of the invitation, but also to the hard work of integration. This is the work of catechesis, which consists, at least, of *orientation*, *inclusion*, and *education*.

Orientation is that process whereby we help strangers learn to negotiate the intricate pathways through which our church life is structured. Most literally, it means introducing those who are new to the variety of ways in which they can participate in the life of our congregation. "These are our opportunities for fellowship, for service, for help with the leadership of worship." "These are the people you should speak with if you are interested in any of these opportunities," or better yet, "these are the people who have already spoken with you to help you discern your interest."

More profoundly, orientation involves introducing those who are new to the spiritual practices of our lives. "This is how we pray, or the variety of ways in which we pray." "This is baptism." "This is confirmation." "This is how we seek healing and forgiveness." It is not enough to proclaim the power of the Spirit if we don't teach those who are new how we've learned to participate in the life of the Spirit.

Inclusion is what brings the stranger from the pathways that they access through our orientation into the rooms of service and fellowship to which these pathways lead. I was wary of using the word "inclusion" here, given its popularized sense. Note in this case that inclusion is directed not so much to a feeling—"we want everyone to feel included"—as it is to an activity and reality. We want to actively include those who come to our tables in the life that we share.

Sara Miles writes powerfully of the effect of the invitation she received at St. Gregory's of Nyssa not just to join everyone at the table, but to join in service at the table, serving a role in the meal. At that moment, she discovered that "you can't be a Christian by yourself."[22] Participation in the mission of the community helped her realize how deeply her life was bound to the life of the community.

Education is the means through which we all learn the gospel context of our fellowship and service so that we might live more fully into it. One concern with the open table is that it neglects catechesis in this narrower sense of educating folks into the gospel. This is to ignore, however, the integral role that catechesis plays in the fullness of hospitality to which opening the table invites us. We haven't been truly hospitable to our guests unless we tell them the stories and share with them the deep learnings of our lives so that they may join us in the journey of the Christian family. Again, you have only truly been invited into a family when you have been offered the stories that have served as the touchstones in the formation of that family.

At the heart of this catechesis is the gospel story of Jesus. We tell this story because we find the grace of God most fully expressed and experienced in this story of God's gift of God's self in Jesus' life, death, and resurrection. We also tell this story, however, for its power to illuminate and conform us to the true structure of love in our lives. It reveals love's paschal mystery—that we find life's fullness only by the gift of ourselves to the other, even as God gave God's self in Jesus. The gospel lies at the heart of our catechesis, then, not simply so that we might teach outsiders our ways but so that we might learn more deeply God's ways in Jesus. Only through the continual baptismal immersion of the Christian community in Jesus' story can it be transformed into a paschal community that reflects the true image of Jesus' love.

Preaching and the Mission of the Church

One implication of opening the table, then, is the demand that it places on preaching the word alongside the celebration of the meal in our Eucharists. However much we can address the evangelical imperative of the church's hospitality in our prayers and our invitation to the table, and however

22. Miles, *Take This Bread*, 96.

much we can address the catechetical imperative through what we do in the classroom, it's clear that a congregation's preaching ministry is essential to its realization of its evangelical and catechetical mission. Indeed, it is more accurate simply to recognize that the evangelism and catechesis offered in prayer, invitation, or classroom are aspects of the church's proclamation, so that they exist in close relationship with what happens from the pulpit (or center aisle) of a congregation on Sunday morning.

The task of the preacher is complex when we recognize the fullness of her or his mission under the impetus of the open table. Many open table congregations allow their commitment to hospitality to shape their proclamation of the word, so that their sermons are open and addressed to those still skeptical of the Christian faith as well as those who have owned it for themselves. They have asked themselves, in other words, how they can preach the gospel to those for whom its language and categories may be foreign. This recalls the evangelical dimension of hospitality discussed above.

At the same time, the catechetical dimension of hospitality demands preaching that will, through its richness, lead the members of a congregation more deeply into the paschal mystery by which they have been embraced. This requires some depth of vision and some complexity in that vision's articulation.

It is a challenge for a preacher to speak to both demands that Jesus' hospitality places on them. How do we proclaim the gospel in a manner that is evangelically accessible but not simplistic, that is catechetically complex and rich but not opaque? Even more, how do we do both together?

This challenge, though demanding, need not be avoided, especially when we recognize that evangelical and catechetical preaching each involves the other. If the evangelical imperative is to powerfully name the grace of God given us in Jesus, then surely a detailed exploration of that grace, an exposition of its richness, its breadth, and its capacity to speak to the fullness of our lives only aids and abets preaching's power. Likewise, our catechetical efforts will be true to the grace in Jesus and the Spirit only if they don't let the surprise of that grace—its capacity to swiftly change our lives—get lost in its rich complexity. Without the surprise, complexity becomes mere complication.

Preaching can manifest the richness and surprise of life with God through a belief in and commitment to encounter—the theme that has wound through this book. The ground of the Christian life is our encounter with Christ and the Spirit, especially at table and font. Insofar as our proclamation of the word is integral to our participation in baptism and Eucharist, so it is essential to the divine encounters that we experience there. Our preaching is the articulation of this encounter—not simply its explanation, but also its catalyst.

This commitment to encounter in our preaching depends on a belief in the reality of the encounter. It is informed by the whole of Jesus' gospel story, remembering especially that the glorified Jesus with whom we dine in the Eucharist is the Jesus of the Gospels who stands with the outcast. The commitment to encounter is open to and expectant of the movement of the Spirit in the life of believers. And as we have seen time and again, it must trust this encounter to God and God's grace and not seek to protect anyone from the crisis precipitated by this grace.

The fruit of such preaching is repentance and thanksgiving, though our preaching is directed, in the first place, to neither of these. Our preaching, again, is directed to our encounter with God though Jesus and the Spirit. From this encounter and the crisis it provokes, our lives will be changed; and from the new life we find in this change, we will be moved to give thanks.

This, again, is the logic of opening the table to all, whether baptized or not. It is at the table that we meet Jesus, and through this meeting we are led into the breezeway of the Spirit. Our preaching stands in service to these life-changing encounters. It incarnates them in word, even as at table and font they are incarnate in sacrament.

Diaconal Hospitality

Returning again to Sara Miles's *Take This Bread*, the center of the book is her work establishing a food pantry at St. Gregory of Nyssa, the open table congregation where she first found Jesus. In fact, the center of her book is the utter coherence she sees between food pantries and open tables as the mission of the church. We only get the latter—what it means to open our liturgical tables—if we get the former: what it means to feed people, to tend to their hunger, to meet their needs.

"Jesus," Miles contends, "was wholly uninterested in Church."[23] Jesus, instead, lived in the rough and lonely places among those who usually found little welcome in proper religious congregations. Jesus was interested in table fellowship with the children of God that he found in those places.

23. Ibid., 179.

Our hospitality has conformed itself to Jesus' hospitality only as we open our tables in a way that tends to those who live in these rough and lonely places.

In my experience, this core dimension of Christian hospitality is best embodied by the Church of the Epiphany in downtown Washington, DC. Most downtown urban churches are peopled largely by commuters from the suburbs; there are few residents within walking distance of a church located in a business district. But the congregants of Epiphany realized that wasn't the case for their parish, if they just opened their eyes. There were innumerable residents in their neighborhood who were hungry for the ministry of the church. It's just that most of them didn't have homes.

So Epiphany's Sunday morning begins early. There is breakfast, served by members of the parish for the first 200 or so hungry souls that make it to their door. (There is a limit to the hospitality they can manage.) There is an hour of Christian education, usually consisting of Bible study and a variety of art projects. And there is a Eucharist led both by the clergy of the church and by the regular members of this early service, some of whom commute in from the suburbs and some of whom come in off the streets. The church also provides shelter on weekdays for those who live on the streets, and noonday concerts for them together with the men and women who work downtown. They've also begun to take Jesus' table out to a local park at lunch on Tuesdays, to share his fellowship in a rough and lonely place.

Epiphany is "lucky," we might say; they're located in a rough and lonely place, in the canyons of an urban downtown. That makes it so much easier to minister to the people of such a place, or maybe it's just better to say to the people of our world. Yet all congregations are called to this ministry. Our hospitality must be diaconal, serving the world in its need. In the context of the open table, what does such service require?

It requires us first to ask what it means to feed people. That's what we're claiming to do at table. It's interesting when we consider the example of Epiphany. They are, in the first place, a case study for why we need to open our tables. Given their ministry of feeding breakfast to the hungry on Sunday mornings, they push the question of what it would mean to invite God's children to the breakfast table but not to Jesus' table. Conversely, though, we must notice that they also ask us the question of what it would mean to ask God's children to Jesus' table, but to neglect to include them at the breakfast table.

There are countless ways that a congregation can tend to feeding the needs of the hungry who surround it. At Epiphany, they serve breakfast. At St. Gregory of Nyssa, they host a food closet at the church. What's noteworthy in both of these examples is that the sharing of food becomes a catalyst to relationship. These congregations don't simply collect or box up food and send it off to those in need at a distance. That's not hospitality. It doesn't open the lives of anyone inside or outside the community to change or to reconciliation.

Diaconal hospitality, in other words, should be coherent with the whole mode of Christian living embodied in the open table. It's not simply about giving away food. It is, rather, about giving ourselves to our brothers and sisters with and through whatever other gifts they might need so that together we might be transformed.

This emphasis on relationship raises a second question of hospitality to the rough and lonely places for open table congregations. It's the question of who hears the invitation to our feast. It's the question of Matthew's Parable of the Wedding Feast, when the host of the feast sends his servants out to bring people in off the streets to fill his table (Matt 22:1–14). For too many open table congregations, there is an invitation to all gathered with the congregation to come forward for our feast, but there is little attention to the fact that everyone gathered pretty much looks the same. Sunday mornings remain the most segregated hour in the United States—segregated by race and by economic and social class. If the church is called to Christ's mission of reconciliation, to bring healing to a world dispersed and scattered by our Babel curse, then surely our work of opening our tables begins not inside our doors, but without, inviting everyone to join our fellowship with Jesus and paying special attention to inviting those from whom we are most alienated by cultural forces.

Conclusion

John Howard Yoder, the Mennonite theologian, has a wonderful short book, *Body Politics*, that explores in depth and detail what it means for a congregation to embody in its life a reconciling mode of living. Yoder envisions a church called to address the alienation and brokenness of the world in concrete and practical ways. He argues that the church's worship, the central activity of its life, needs to engage directly the world's distorted ways of living. In a fascinating way, Yoder comes from the opposite side of the liturgical spectrum from someone like Schmemann (one of our guides throughout this book), yet he would agree with Schmemann's concern that we not allow a sacred barrier to stand between our worship and the rest of our ecclesial life or the life of the world.

For Yoder, our worship life should order the *polis* of the church, the life of our community, even as the life of our community should stand as a transformative icon for the *polis* of the world. This insight challenges congregations of all stripes within the church. It is the challenge to actually live the reconciliation that we preach, to take seriously Jesus' primary concern not with proper religious congregations, but with the rough and lonely places, and to recognize and acknowledge our foolhardy attempts to box up God, keeping the power of the divine safely sequestered from our day-to-day activities.

This insight—a declaration that the missional imperative of the church should in some sense order the church's worship—neither belongs to open table congregations, nor does it challenge only them. But it does, quite simply, highlight the intuitive case for this practice. It helps us to recognize that the practice of the open table not only addresses this imperative, serving as a means through which our worship embodies the church's reconciling mission in the world, but it also serves as an organizing principle for this imperative. To practice the open table is to organize the *polis* of the church in and around the reality of God's hospitality embodied in the fellowship of Jesus, and it is to offer this *polis*, this embodied hospitality, as a concrete reconciling practice to an alienated and broken world.

The practice of the open table, in other words, has standing as a rite of the church, a mode of Christian living, or, to borrow another of Kavanaugh's phrases, "the way that the redeemed world is done." The practice of closing or gating the table, however, seems to function more as a rubric. It exists as an exception to the church's work of redemption, a pause from that work so that the workers may have a moment to take sustenance before they return to their mission. A priest whom I know and respect announces at his dismissal from the Eucharist, "Now the worship has ended; let the service begin." This, I think, is a succinct encapsulation of the practice of the closed table. It is a practice of worship that stands apart from our service to or mission in the world, even as it envisions our mission and service apart from our worship.

Whatever else the practice of the open table might mean, it means principally to envision mission and worship together. The church's mission and worship are centered on, driven by, and directed toward our fellowship with Jesus. At table, we meet Jesus and are transformed by him. At table, the Spirit blows. At table, the world is reconciled. To open our tables is simply to invite the world, our neighbors, our friends to Jesus, the Spirit, and God's reconciliation. To open our tables is really as simple as that. Know, however, that with that invitation it will demand the whole of our lives.

Bibliography

Augustine. *The Confessions of St. Augustine*. Translated by John K. Ryan. New York: Image, 1960.

Bauman, Zygmunt. *Community: Seeking Safety in an Insecure World*. Cambridge: Polity, 2001.

Beasley-Murray, G. R. *Baptism in the New Testament*. London: MacMillan, 1962.

Borg, Marcus. *Meeting Jesus Again for the First Time: The Historical Jesus and the Heart of Contemporary Faith*. New York: HarperOne, 1995.

Bradshaw, Paul. *Eucharistic Origins*. London: SPCK, 2004.

———. *Reconstructing Early Christian Worship*. Collegeville, MN: Liturgical, 2009.

Brown, Raymond. *The Churches the Apostles Left Behind*. New York: Paulist, 1984.

Calvin, John. *Commentaries on the Book of Genesis*. Vol. I. Translated by John King. Grand Rapids: Baker, 2003.

———. *Institutes of the Christian Religion*. Library of Christian Classics, vol. 20. Translated by Ford Lewis Battles. Philadelphia: Westminster, 1960.

Chrysostom, John. *Baptismal Instructions*. Ancient Christian Writers. Translated by Paul W. Harkins. Edited by Johannes Quasten and Walter J. Burghardt, S. J. London: Longman, Green, 1963.

Cohen, Anthony. *The Symbolic Construction of Community*. New York: Routledge, 1985.

Crossan, John Dominic. *The Historical Jesus: The Life of a Mediterranean Jewish Peasant*. San Francisco: HarperSanFrancisco, 1991.

———. *Jesus: A Revolutionary Biography*. San Francisco: HarperOne, 1994.

Cyprian of Carthage. *The Letters of St. Cyprian of Carthage*. Vol. 3. Ancient Christian Writers. Translated by G. W. Clarke. Edited by Johannes Quasten and Walter J. Burghardt, S. J. New York: Newman, 1986.

Dix, Dom Gregory. *The Shape of the Liturgy*. New York: Seabury, 1983.

Edmondson, Stephen. *Calvin's Christology*. Cambridge: Cambridge University Press, 2004.

———. "Opening the Table: The Body of Christ and God's Prodigal Grace." *Anglican Theological Review* 91:2 (Spring 2009) 213–34.

Farb, Peter, and George Armelagos. *Consuming Passions: The Anthropology of Eating*. Boston: Houghton Mifflin, 1980.

Fabian, Richard. "First the Table, Then the Font." http://www.saintgregorys.org/Resources_pdfs/FirsttheTable.pdf.

Farwell, James. "Baptism, Eucharist, and the Hospitality of Jesus: On the Practice of 'Open Communion.'" *Anglican Theological Review* 86:2 (Spring 2004) 215–38.

Feeley-Harnik, Gillian. *The Lord's Table: Eucharist and Passover in Early Christianity*. Philadelphia: University of Pennsylvania Press, 1981.

Greene-McCreight, Kathryn. "'We Are Companions of the Patriarchs' or Scripture Absorbs Calvin's World." *Modern Theology* 14:2 (1998) 213–24.

Hippolytus. *The Treatise on the Apostolic Tradition of St. Hippolytus of Rome*. Edited by Gregory Dix. London: SPCK, 1968.

Hooker, Richard. *Of the Lawes of Ecclesiasticall Politie*. Book V. The Fogler Library Edition of the Works of Richard Hooker. Edited by W. Speed Hill. London: Belknap, 1977.

Johnson, Luke Timothy. *The Gospel of Luke*. Collegeville, MN: Liturgical, 2006.

———. *The Real Jesus: The Misguided Quest for the Historical Jesus and the Truth of the Traditional Gospels*. San Francisco: HarperSanFrancisco, 1996.

Jones, Serene. *Feminist Theory and Christian Theology: Cartographies of Grace*. Minneapolis: Fortress, 2000.

Karris, Robert. *Luke: Artist and Theologian*. Mahwah, NJ: Paulist, 1985.

Kavanaugh, Aidan. *On Liturgical Theology*. Collegeville, MN: Liturgical, 1981.

———. *The Shape of Baptism: The Rite of Christian Initiation*. Collegeville, MN: Liturgical, 1991.

Klosinski, Lee Edward. *The Meals in Mark*. Ann Arbor, MI: University Microfilms, 1988.

Lathrop, Gordon. *Holy People: A Liturgical Ecclesiology*. Minneapolis: Fortress, 1999.

———. *Holy Things: A Liturgical Theology*. Minneapolis: Fortress, 1993.

Leon-Dufour, Xavier. *Sharing the Eucharistic Bread: The Witness of the New Testament*. Mahwah, NJ: Paulist, 1987.

Marshall, Paul. "Additional Notes." In Dom Gregory Dix, *The Shape of the Liturgy*, 765–77. New York: Seabury, 1983.

Martyn, J. Louis. *History and Theology in the Fourth Gospel*. Louisville: Westminster John Knox, 2003.

Meeks, Wayne. *The First Urban Christians: The Social World of the Apostle Paul*. New Haven: Yale University Press, 1983.

Merton, Thomas. *The Seven Storey Mountain: An Autobiography of Faith*. New York: Harcourt, Brace, 1998.

Miles, Sara. *Take This Bread: A Radical Conversion*. New York: Ballantine: 2007.

Putnam, Robert. *Bowling Alone: The Collapse and Revival of American Community*. New York: Simon and Schuster, 2000.

Richard of St. Victor. *Richard of St. Victor*. The Classics of Western Spirituality. Translated by Grover Zinn. New York: Paulist, 1979.

Ricoeur, Paul. *Oneself As Another*. Chicago: University of Chicago, 1992.

Schmemann, Alexander. *The Eucharist*. Crestwood, NY: St. Valdimir's Seminary Press, 1987.

———. *For the Life of the World*. Crestwood, NY: St. Vladimir's Seminary Press, 2002.

———. *Of the Water and the Spirit: A Liturgical Study of Baptism*. Crestwood, NY: St. Vladimir's Seminary Press, 1997.

———. *On Liturgical Theology*. Crestwood, NY: St. Vladimir's Seminary Press, 1966.

Stamm, Mark. *Let Every Soul Be Jesus' Guest: A Theology of the Open Table*. Nashville: Abingdon, 2006.

Theology Committee of the House of Bishops of the Episcopal Church. "Reflections on Holy Baptism and the Holy Eucharist: A Response to Resolution D084 of the 75th General Convention." *Anglican Theological Review* 93:1 (Winter 2011) 1–8.

Wainwright, Geoffrey. *Eucharist and Eschatology*. Akron, OH: OSL Publications, 2002.

Wrede, William. *The Messianic Secret*. Translated by J. C. G. Greig. Cambridge: James Clark: 1971.

Yoder, John Howard. *Body Politics: Five Practices of the Christian Community Before the Watching World.* Nashville: Discipleship Resources, 1992.

Zizioulas, John. *Being As Communion: Studies in Personhood and the Church.* Crestwood, NY: St. Vladimir's Seminary Press, 1997.

Made in the USA
Lexington, KY
14 May 2016